# Vaghaar

# Vaghaar

A Gujarati Cookbook
Indian Recipes From my Mother's Kitchen

Alissa Lad

Smith Street Books

Mum, me and Maa (Manjulaben), 1990s

For my mum, Mina,
and all the talented cooks in my family.

Your delicious food is the inspiration for this book.

Contents

**Contents**

# Introduction

My mum has always told me my eyes are bigger than my belly. For as long as I can remember, I've been an indulgent eater, and I've especially loved Mum's home cooking. Still today, eating her food evokes vivid memories of my childhood, including the weekly schedule – veg curry on a Monday and Tuesday, meat curry on a Wednesday and 'Western' food for the rest of the week.

Despite this, it wasn't until I spent five months back at home during the pandemic, well into my 20s, that I realised I couldn't cook any of my mum's beloved Gujarati food. After I first moved out of home for university, I had unconsciously settled into the routine of missing out on those cherished tastes of home until my next return visit. Each time a trip home was approaching, the subtle anticipation of what home-cooked food lay ahead simmered in the back of my mind, and I always had my first meal request ready: kidney bean nu shaak (kidney bean curry).

Eating Indian food was so routine during childhood, it never occurred to me that I could prepare these meals myself. I realise now that I took Mum's food for granted. It took a re-entering into the regular enjoyment of her cooking for me to realise that I needed to learn her myriad internal recipes and techniques – not just for my own enjoyment, but to reconnect with an essential part of my family history and cultural heritage. These family recipes have been passed down for generations and endured migration across continents, from India and Kenya to the UK. I felt a strong, growing urge to understand where my culture came from and to play an active role in where it is going.

This new aspiration hit a stumbling block pretty much immediately: Mum did all her cooking from memory. Recipes were never written down in my family, only passed on verbally and taught from a very young age. With both parents out at work and being the eldest sister, Mum first started cooking at the age of nine. Now, everything is instinctual, cemented in her memory like a native language. This posed a problem – there was no chance I could memorise the countless dishes in the same way. I needed to write them down, and it would be for the first time. As I began the process, an exciting idea appeared: a cookbook documenting the Gujarati recipes from my mum, grandmas and the other talented women in my family.

For someone who loves food so much, cooking was not my passion. To be honest, I didn't particularly enjoy being in the kitchen, and before undertaking this project I would consider myself a mediocre cook. I'm a designer at heart and have been fortunate enough to build a career doing what I love. Ever since I started studying and working in graphic design, it's been a goal of mine to design a book. Having the freedom to experiment and creatively express my vision across the pages here, through typography and film photography, has been an absolute dream. I've never had any professional culinary training. But then, neither has my mum, nor anyone else in my family – but they have all contributed to the amazing dishes you'll find here. This is reflective of the essence of *Vaghaar*: at its core, this is earnest, wholesome, simple (for the most part) home cooking.

These pages contain not only recipes, but document my learning process as well. In 2022, I moved to Melbourne and truly loved the time I spent there, as most do it seems. But, moving so far away proved to be a big incentive to get this project underway, as it forced me to hone my ability to cook Mum's food. It was the perfect way to feel closer to home through the senses of taste and smell. This book is a celebration of my culture and my mum's delicious food. It's for those like me who grew up eating Gujarati food but never learnt how to cook it. It's for anyone wanting to discover Indian food from a different region; beyond the flavours of a standard British Indian takeaway. I hope this book provides encouragement and the knowledge that it's never too late to learn how to cook a new cuisine and, more importantly, it's never too late to reconnect with your roots – and help new branches to grow.

Melton Road, Belgrave, Leicester

I'm a second-generation Gujarati Indian, born and raised in Leicester, a city in the East Midlands, which is home to the highest concentration of South Asians in the UK. The story of Gujarati heritage in the UK follows one of two paths: migration directly from the motherland to the UK or by way of East Africa. For me, it's both. Mum's family came from Gujarat and settled in and around Bradford and Dad's family came from Kenya and resettled in Leicester (though they, too, were born in Gujarat before migrating first to Nairobi). This convergence has made for a potent blend of Indian culture with East African and now British influences.

The late 1960s and early 1970s saw a new wave of migration to the UK, due in part to the 'Africanisation' policies of several East African countries that were newly independent from colonial rule. Drastic economic changes in Kenya resulted in a lot of East African Asians leaving, as was the case for my Maa (grandma) and Dada (grandad) on my dad's side. They, among many others in the same boat, became 'twice migrants'. Being British passport holders with existing community ties to cities like Leicester meant that moving to the UK became the best option for the pursuit of a better life for the family. Many of them relocated to the areas of Melton Road, Rushey Mead and Belgrave. Leicester now proudly hosts the biggest Diwali celebration outside of India, and Melton Road has been vibrantly transformed into the Golden Mile, populated end-to-end with Indian eateries, grocery shops, and sari and jewellery shops. Truly a Little India.

While it may not be your typical must-see tourist destination in the UK, I would highly recommend a visit if you are travelling from overseas (or if you live in the UK and haven't been!). Admittedly, I have my own bias, but the rich cultural impact immigration has had on the city is difficult to describe. It must be experienced. You will find a range of South Asian cuisines from Gujarati, Punjabi, Sri Lankan, Bengali and Indo-Chinese. Eateries like Chai Paani, Bobby's, Indian Rooster and Tangoe are just a few of my favourites that I'd recommend. You can find places like Paddy's Marten Inn where two of Britain's most beloved customs meet: pubs and quality Indian food. Their sizzling mixed grill is a must-try. I'd also recommend picking up some Indian sweets (which you won't find in this book) such as jalebi, burfi, laddu, gulab jamun and raas malai, which are a few of my favourites. Beware though, there are seemingly no limits when it comes to sweetness, so only indulge if you have a sweet tooth.

For all the benefits immigration brought to us Brits, migrating here in the 1960s and 1970s was not an easy process. My grandparents found themselves in a cold, alien, unwelcoming environment. The strong and often cruel social pressure to 'fit in' in order for their family to prosper meant their own culture was gradually diluted. Christmas became a bigger celebration than Diwali. Mum and Dad could speak Gujarati, but didn't learn to read or write it. My sister and I could somewhat understand it, but only speak a handful of words and phrases. Unfortunately, our parents spoke to us almost exclusively in English, although food was a bit of an exception, and I grew up only knowing the Gujarati word for a lot of the dishes that I've included here. I only knew aubergine as 'ringan', lentils as 'daal', and okra, or lady fingers, as 'bhinda'. Later in life, I learnt that the version of Gujarati I knew was in fact laced with Swahili. For example, I knew sahani as 'plate' in Gujarati, though it is actually a Swahili word.

Despite the hardship, both my grandparents found their feet and fought for a better life for us. Stereotypically, Maa and Dada on Mum's side owned an off-licence, where the customers nicknamed Dada 'Jimmy' – the name Ranchhodbhai was unfamiliar and difficult to remember. He didn't have much say in this, but it made him feel part of the community.

Mum did try her best to teach me and my sister to cook in the same way my maa taught her, but regrettably I wasn't interested. It was a part of my identity that I had unknowingly repressed, which left me feeling disconnected as an adult. Upon reflection, I felt that an echo of what my grandparents felt back then reverberated within me, two generations later. Thankfully, I didn't face any racism, but I didn't feel connected to my culture. Other than through food, that is. Food has always been the strongest connection to my roots.

Having lived in London, Singapore and Melbourne since leaving home, I've been truly spoiled by the exceptional worldly cuisines these foodie destinations have to offer, and my love for food has only grown. Still, nothing can beat a good home-cooked Gujarati meal. Spending time away, I was able to appreciate the diverse beauty of my community in a new light and better understand the immeasurable ways the Indian diaspora has contributed to British life. This was punctuated by my experience travelling to India for the first time at the age of 22. I knew that my sense of belonging remained in the Midlands, stemming from the collision of British and Indian cultures.

Dada (Nanubhai) in Kenya, 1950s

The Lad family loves to eat, we often say it's in our genes. It's impossible to visit Maa and Dada's house without being fed most of the contents of their fridge or cupboard and leaving with a whole bag of groceries. You come home looking like you've just been to the supermarket. Food functions as the nucleus for most of our gatherings, which typically involve an all-day eating affair with everyone bringing a dish.

Maa's daar bhat (daal with rice) is a family favourite, as was my late dada's infamous yet beloved lamb curry, which he loved to cook in bulk on his makeshift garage stove for special occasions – a set-up that definitely wouldn't meet today's safety standards. The curry was too oily and too spicy, but everyone would always go back for more. Mum has tried numerous times to emulate these recipes, but they are never quite the same. It is comforting to know that my mum has the same difficulty trying to reproduce these dishes that I do with hers. There really is an indefinable quality, a magic touch that gets lost, or maybe renewed, across each generation.

Food really is Mum's love language. Whenever I visit home, she will still text me the day before to ask what I'd like to eat, guaranteed. What she's cooking next and who she's cooking for is always on her mind. Cooking for a big family get-together – something that can send many people into a meltdown – is therapeutic for her. She takes pleasure in everyone coming together and sharing her delicious food.

Writing these recipes down wasn't just difficult because she did everything by eye; it also didn't help that Mum is naturally experimental. It's always been a little bit of this, a little bit of that, sometimes add this in, sometimes don't. Her texts and bare-boned handwritten recipes can be found throughout the book. They demonstrate the undertaking I had in transcribing the recipes for a cookbook, but I like to think their minimal form expresses the personal nature of each recipe, how her own indefinable touch is in every dish. The evidence is in the taste. I'll admit, I've never been able to get them exactly the same, but now I've been able to make them my own and you can do so, too.

Personalisation is an important part of the ethos. I like to use more garlic and lemon than Mum. I also eat meat much less frequently and, as I'm lactose intolerant, I've ended up with a mostly vegan diet. The recipes in this book reflect that, being heavier on the veg side of things, and are also representative of the cuisine in mainland Gujarat, which is primarily vegetarian. That said, meat is a big part of the British diet, so it was important to include the meat dishes I grew up with too. The intertwinement of culture and migration is captured in this food – Mum has always cooked in a British household and that's undoubtedly made an imprint on the evolution of the dishes. She's definitely partial to a bit of Heinz tomato ketchup with an Indian meal. Anyway, the point is that the contents of this book can be shaped to your tastes, so work with what you like and what food you've got in your cupboard and fridge. Experimentation is always encouraged.

In Gujarat, different regions and castes cook the same dishes in different ways. Most of my extended family are from Navsari and the surrounding areas, but these recipes are merely a window into Gujarati cooking in a British household, and are not fully representative of all the wonderful dishes to come out of the region. The dishes in this book are the meals that I've grown up with and which I truly believe can be enjoyed by anyone willing to give them a try.

Learning to cook most of these recipes while I was living in Melbourne was my home-away-from-home comfort. As is the case for so many of us, no one can match up to Mum's cooking. If I can reach even a fraction of her ability and open the door for others to do the same, I will consider it a success!

Indo mie
Instant Noodles
40+2 packs Free Inside
Chicken Flavor
More Love
NEXTURE
Oberveg
RIPE PLANTAINE
3 FOR £1
CASI Gourmet
Plantains

## Documented on Film

All the photographs in this book were captured on my Canon Z135, a simple, easy to use point-and-shoot film camera that I got secondhand for £30. As with cooking itself, the process of collecting, transcribing and testing the recipes in this book was an imperfect one with plenty of trial and error. Abstaining from the abundance and selectivity that is inherent in digital photography, I've aimed to capture this process with the honesty of analogue. Film can also cast some ambiguity around the era in which a picture is taken; the format itself provides a nostalgic air, while the content within the picture may contradict that. It is not entirely here nor there, and with this I hope the imagery can match the cross-generational and timeless quality of the food itself. Different curries often look alike when finished and are not the most attractive meals to photograph, so you'll also see a mix of fresh foods, kitchen workspaces, shopping environments, dinner parties and lots of hands. Hands are essential for eating curry!

The absence of a 'perfect' image for every recipe is intended to encourage individual experimentation and reject the idea of a singular, ideal finished product. I wanted to photograph sincere and accessible home cooking and the images are a window into my own journey reconnecting with this important pillar of my family history. The food here is made to be shared and that aspect is also highlighted in the photography. You'll see an array of kitchens in which these recipes were written, tested and photographed, where I'm either learning new recipes from Mum, Maa and my many aunties, or cooking a spread for friends while taking advantage of their amenities (not to mention moving house three times during the making of this book).

## The Art of Vaghaar

The possibilities of a curry are endless. A traditional homemade curry starts with the same foundation, the vaghaar. Known as 'tempering' in English, vaghaar is the technique of frying off a mix of spices to release their aromas and infuse the oil, creating a layer of flavour that is then absorbed by the main ingredients. Knowing what combination of spices to use is one of the most important skills in Indian cooking. Once this process is understood, it unlocks a vast potential for experimentation.

The distinct smell of a vaghaar is so fragrant that it clings to your clothes and seeps through the walls, always informing passers-by and neighbours of what you've been up to in the kitchen. Underscoring almost all the recipes, *Vaghaar* felt like an appropriate choice for a title that succinctly embodies the essence of the book.

Tel

*Oil*

Rye

*Black Mustard Seeds*

Jeeru

*Cumin Seeds*

Methi

*Fenugreek*

Tuj

*Cinnamon Stick*

Lavinga

*Clove*

Elaichi

*Cardamom*

Ajwain

*Carom Seeds*

Hing

*Asafoetida*

RAJ
Tandoori Masala
BORWICK'S
Baking Powder
17

# Cookbook Notes

## Spices

Always add a heaped teaspoon of ground coriander and ground cumin. You can never add too much of either.

Add salt to taste. I don't like my food too salty, so 1 teaspoon is enough for me. I find meat dishes tend to need more salt.

Add chilli to taste. I keep the seeds in when using chilli, but you can remove the seeds for less spice. Many recipes use 1 fresh green chilli and ½–1 teaspoon of ground red chilli, however, feel free to add more or less. Sometimes, if I'm craving a spicy dish, I'll add an extra fresh chilli.

If you have one to hand, use a food processor to blitz fresh spices like garlic, ginger and chilli – it will save you time.

Another handy tip is to freeze ice-cube blocks of garlic and ginger paste and chilli paste separately (as the chilli amounts differ in some recipes). Blitz together equal measures of garlic and ginger and add to the holes of an ice-cube tray. Do the same with chillies. They will keep frozen for up to 4 months.

A masala dabba is a staple in many Indian households. It's a metal tin containing six to eight small pots that hold essential spices, keeping them easily accessible when cooking (especially since most dry spices are added at the same time). Common spices include black mustard seeds, ground coriander, ground cumin, ground turmeric, garam masala, fenugreek, cinnamon sticks and ground red chilli.

## Cooking Tips

Always use fresh tomatoes where possible.

When making the vaghaar, fry until you start to hear a slight pop or sizzle, or until you start to smell the aroma from the spices. This is how you know your vaghaar is ready – you don't want to burn it.

If your curry sauce starts to dry out, add a splash of water. This may happen when you simmer the tomatoes, which is a common step when making a curry.

When your bread gets stale or is on its last legs, blitz it up into breadcrumbs and freeze them. You can use them for *Spicy Crumbs Chicken* (page 104) or *Keema Scotch Eggs* (page 108).

You can add spinach to pretty much any curry to bulk it out.

## Substitutions

I use olive oil but you can use your oil of choice. My mum prefers to use canola (rapeseed) oil or ghee. If using a nut oil, such as coconut, be wary as this could change the flavour of the food. I recommend always using sunflower or vegetable oil for deep-frying.

Indian cooking usually has a lot of oil in it (which is what makes it tasty), so feel free to cook with more oil. Vegetable dishes usually require more oil.

Ghee is commonly used instead of oil. It is clarified butter, rich in vitamins with anti-inflammatory properties. It also has a high smoke point, which is great for cooking on high heat. People who cannot tolerate dairy are often able to tolerate ghee because of the absence of the casein and proteins found in butter. It can also be used to moisturise the skin and hair!

As I am dairy intolerant, I have tested all these recipes with dairy alternatives to yoghurt, butter and milk. I will state when you can use a dairy-free alternative. I often use coconut-based yoghurt, vegan butter and oat or almond milk. Be wary that dairy alternatives often have added ingredients that may change the cooking time or texture. I prefer Coco Collab brand coconut-based yoghurt and Flora vegan butter, but you can use whatever you prefer.

Followers of Jainism don't cook with onion or garlic for religious reasons and I know the FODMAP diet often suggests removing these from your diet (as they are part of the amaryllis family) for bloating and digestion reasons. As alternatives, I would use garlic-infused oil and leeks or green onion (the green part of the spring onion/scallion).

## Serving Suggestions

Enjoy any curry with *Everyday Rotli* (page 195). We usually eat rotli with every Indian meal and it is a treat if we have another form of bread or rice. You can always cheat and use store-bought rotli or rice.

Bread is also a great alternative when you haven't made enough rotlis but still need to scrape up the remaining curry sauce.

Make a toastie with any dry curry and cheese – it's the perfect next-day lunch! Get creative – nearly anything can go in between two pieces of bread.

Everyone loves a pastry. Any curry – dry or wet – tastes delicious encased inside puff pastry.

Cool the spice with yoghurt. If anything is too spicy, add a spoonful of yoghurt or pair it with *Cooling Raita* (page 230) or *Mint Yoghurt* (page 231).

We accompany most of our Indian meals with store-bought papad (poppadum), which we cook in the microwave (which is much healthier than frying, although the fried version is always a nice treat).

We also use store-bought mango chutney and aubergine (eggplant) chutney, which nicely accompanies most vegetarian dishes.

## The Recipes

This book uses a 15 ml (½ fl oz) tablespoon.

All oven temperatures given are for a fan-forced oven. If using a conventional oven, increase the temperature by 20°C (70°F).

CRUNCHY
EANS
LOVING LOCAL

## Get-Togethers

On the following pages, you'll find a selection of menu ideas that I hope will provide some inspiration for when you've got a few extra mouths to feed or are looking to put on a spread. Whether it's a lavish dinner party or a simple weekday meal, the dishes in these menus complement each other nicely – at least in my experience of countless family get-togethers!

The Saturday-night spread is for when you want to impress. You'll need a full day for it, but it's a great opportunity to enjoy the social and mindful benefits that a long stint in the kitchen can offer. Make sure your guests arrive on an empty stomach. If you're hosting a brunch, try spicing it up with a *Masala Shakshuka* (page 83), best served with sliced sourdough bread and orange juice. At home, we'd always follow this with *Morning Masala Chai* (page 49) and a small sweet treat like nankhatai.

The weekday menus give a rough idea of what my week looked like growing up in the Lad household, although we often had more Western cuisine in the latter half of the week. Typically, we have rotli with every meal, sometimes followed by a second course of rice. These are all delicious, quick dishes – try completing the full week if you want to challenge (and treat) yourself.

## The All-Out Saturday Dinner Party

Vegetarian/ Vegan
6–8 People

---

### Snacks & Small Plates

| | |
|---|---|
| Easy Bombay Mix | p. 58 |
| Baked Handvo | p. 72 |
| Mixed Veg Bhajis | p. 78 |

### Curries

| | |
|---|---|
| Heart-Warming Daal | p. 130 |
| Matar Paneer *or* | p. 139 |
| Creamy Chana nu Shaak (for vegan) | p. 136 |

### Breads & Rice

| | |
|---|---|
| Poori | p. 196 |
| Plain basmati rice (with a spoonful of butter/vegan butter mixed through it) | |

### Condiments

| | |
|---|---|
| Tomato Chutney | p. 233 |
| Fresh Green Chutney | p. 234 |
| Coconut Chutney | p. 236 |

### Dessert

| | |
|---|---|
| Creamy Doodhpak (made using a plant-based milk for vegan) | p. 248 |

## The All-Out Saturday Dinner Party

Meat & Vegetables
6–8 People

---

### Snacks & Small Plates


| | |
|---|---|
| Easy Bombay Mix | p. 58 |
| Spicy Pea Pastries | p. 85 |
| Tray-Baked Lamb Chops | p. 114 |


### Curries


| | |
|---|---|
| Heart-Warming Chicken Curry | p. 166 |
| Spicy Lemon Salmon | p. 179 |
| Bhaji nu Shaak | p. 157 |


### Breads & Rice


| | |
|---|---|
| Everyday Rotli | p. 195 |
| Vaghaar Rice | p. 210 |


### Condiments


| | |
|---|---|
| Tomato Chutney | p. 233 |
| Mint Yoghurt | p. 231 |
| Pickled Onions | p. 237 |


### Dessert


| | |
|---|---|
| Gajar na Halwa | p. 256 |

## Brunch
## With Friends

4 People

### Drinks



### Snacks & Small Plates



### Dessert

## Quick, Wholesome Weekday Dinners

4 People

---

### Monday

#### Curries

Monday Kidney Bean nu Shaak p. 126

#### Breads & Rice

Everyday Rotli p. 195

Quick Vegetable Rice p. 213

---

### Tuesday

#### Curries

Ringan Palita nu Shaak p. 145

#### Breads & Rice

Plain basmati rice
(with a spoonful of butter/vegan butter mixed through it)

#### Condiments & Sauces

Maa's Daal p. 241

## Quick, Wholesome Weekday Dinners

4 People

---

### Wednesday

#### Curries



#### Breads & Rice



Plain basmati rice
(with a spoonful of butter/vegan butter mixed through it)

#### Condiments & Sauces



---

### Thursday

#### Curries



#### Breads & Rice

## Quick, Wholesome Weekday Dinners

4 People

### Friday

#### Small Plates

Versatile Salad p. 118

#### Curries

Jinga p. 175

Fish Curry p. 178

#### Condiments & Sauces

Yoghurt Naan Bread p. 198

Plain basmati rice
(with a spoonful of butter/vegan butter mixed through it)

## Home-Grown Tomatoes

Tomatoes feature heavily in this book and are the foundational ingredient for a lot of the recipes. I would encourage people to grow whatever vegetables they have the means to, but tomatoes are particularly good for growing yourself because they don't require too much time and effort. Dad grows his own in our family garden and they've always tasted sweeter than the ones you buy at the supermarket. Don't worry if you don't have a garden – you can grow tomatoes indoors. (An office I used to work in even had a few indoor tomato plants on the go!) Growing your own is a great way to source fresher, more environmentally friendly ingredients on the cheap.

Here's a basic guide on how to grow tomatoes, both indoors and out. It will get you started regardless of whether or not you've got a green thumb. Who knows, maybe it could be the start of a new horticultural obsession?

**Note**

The monthly timings are based on UK seasons (Northern Hemisphere) with the corresponding Southern Hemisphere seasons given in parentheses.

**Cordon (indeterminate)**

These are fast growing tomato plants that need suitably tall supports. They take up very little ground space.

**Bush (determinate)**

Bush tomato plants are more compact, making them great for smaller spaces. They are easier to grow, with little maintenance required.

## Step 1
## Choose Your Seeds or Seedlings

**February–March (August–September)**

Choose a tomato variety (cherry, plum, salad, etc.).

Beginners will find seedlings from a garden centre easier to grow than starting from seed.

If starting from seed, sow seeds indoors for greenhouse plants. Keep at 18°C (64°F) with good light. They will generally crop earlier if using a greenhouse.

**March–April (September–October)**

Sow seeds for outdoor plants. Place on a warm windowsill and cover with a clear plastic bag to maintain humidity. Seedlings should appear within 2 weeks.

## Step 2
## Potting & Planting

**April–May (October–November)**

After 2 weeks, the seedlings should have a couple of leaves. Re-pot them into individual pots using peat-free multi-purpose compost. Keep the pots at a temperature of 16°C (60°F) in a bright place.

**May–June (November–December)**

Outdoors: Choose a sunny spot with at least 6–8 hours of direct sunlight. Move the plants to their final position once temperatures outside are above 16°C (60°F). You can plant them in large containers or growing bags in a greenhouse or outdoors in the ground, making sure to add plenty of garden compost prior – tomatoes like loose, well-drained soil. Plant the seedlings deep, covering the stem and the first set of leaves.

Indoors: Use pots at least 30 cm (12 in) deep with good drainage and place them near a bright, sunny window.

## Step 3
## Plant care

**June–August (December–February)**

Water the tomato plants regularly at the base of the plant to keep the soil/compost moist.

Use a tomato fertiliser or balanced plant food every 2–3 weeks once flowers appear.

Support the plants as they grow. Cordon tomatoes will need tall supports, while bush tomatoes will only require support if they grow quite large.

Remove any side shoots from cordon tomatoes. Bush tomatoes should be left to grow without pruning.

## Step 4
## Harvesting

**July–September (January–March)**

The tomatoes are ready when they are fully coloured, firm and come away easily from the stem. Harvest regularly to encourage more fruiting.

Cherry tomatoes ripen more quickly than larger tomatoes.

Greenhouse plants usually start cropping earlier than those outdoors.

**October (April)**

At the end of the season, pick the remaining green fruit to ripen indoors before any frost appears.

# Drinks

*Peevanu*

Other than the essential daily cup of chai, Indian drinks aren't regularly consumed in our household. However, my dad, who lived in Kenya until he was five, remembers my maa making him a cold, refreshing glass of yoghurt chaas for those all-year-round summer days, and haldi doodh, a natural remedy for sore throats. Maa is an expert in natural remedies!

# Morning Masala Chai

Serves 2

In our household, chai is an essential morning ritual that my parents can't start the day without, much like coffee for a lot of people. This can be made more fiery with extra ginger, or freshened up with a few mint leaves. Serve with your favourite dunking biscuits – I'd recommend a classic British digestive or something more traditional such as *Nankhatai* (page 259) or saker para, which you can find in most Indian grocery stores.

## Ingredients

2–3 cm (¾–1¼ in) piece of ginger, grated

1½ teaspoons loose black tea

½ teaspoon tea masala mix (see Notes)

a few mint leaves (optional)

250–300 ml (8½–10 fl oz) milk or plant-based milk

sugar, to taste (optional)

biscuits (cookies), to serve (optional)

## Method

Add 250–300 ml (8½–10 fl oz) of water to a saucepan along with the ginger, tea, pre-mixed tea masala and mint, if using. Stir and bring to the boil.

Once boiling, add the milk and reduce the heat to low. Allow the tea to simmer for 4–5 minutes.

Pour the tea through a fine-mesh sieve into two mugs to serve. Add sugar, if using, and serve hot with your favourite biscuits.

**Notes**

I recommend using the Jalpur brand tea masala mix, though there are lots of brands out there!

Create your own tea masala mix by combining equal amounts of ground ginger and cinnamon with a sprinkle of ground black pepper, white pepper, cardamom, cloves and nutmeg.

# Yoghurt Chaas

Serves 2

This is a classic, yoghurt-based Indian drink that my dad grew up drinking. Refreshing and light, with a hint of cumin, it's perfect for a summer's day.

## Ingredients

200–300 g (7–10½ oz) plain or coconut-based yoghurt (see Note)

ice cubes

200–250 ml (7–8½ fl oz) cold water (see Note)

1 teaspoon ground cumin

pinch of salt, to taste

## Method

Divide the yoghurt between two glasses and add a handful of ice.

Top up the glasses with the cold water. Divide the ground cumin between the glasses and add the salt.

Stir thoroughly and serve ice cold.

**Note**

The quantity of yoghurt and cold water you will need is dependent on the size of glass you use – just be sure to keep the ratio of yoghurt to water at roughly 1:1.

# Haldi Doodh

(Turmeric Milk)

Serves 2

Turmeric – the golden spice. Indians have been using turmeric for its natural health benefits for thousands of years. This healing beverage is the perfect cure for a sore throat and tickly cough.

## Ingredients

250–300 ml (8½–10 fl oz) milk or plant-based milk

1 teaspoon ground turmeric (see Note)

1 teaspoon honey

pinch of salt

## Method

Bring the milk to boiling point in a small saucepan over medium–low heat, then reduce the heat to a simmer. Stir in the remaining ingredients and simmer for 3–4 minutes.

Divide between two mugs and serve hot.

**Note**

If using fresh turmeric, peel and grate 2.5 cm (1 in) of the root and simmer for 1–2 minutes longer.

# Snacks

*Nasto*

‘Nasto’ translates to ‘savoury snack’ in Gujarati. It’s rare to visit an Indian household where you’re not greeted with something to nibble on. To be frank, word would get around if your guests weren’t greeted with any food and drink. While I always encourage making dishes to be shared, nothing quite beats raiding the cupboards for a sneaky nasto when no one’s around. Anytime the Lad family travels abroad, you can be sure we’ll have nasto with us. As much as we love trying new cuisines, home comforts, such as Bombay mix, will always be essential.

# Easy Bombay Mix

Serves 2

This super easy recipe is perfect for a quick snack, or for when unexpected guests pop over. The crunch of the raw onion and zing of the lemon balance out the saltiness of the Bombay mix, creating a delicious combination of flavours and textures. It has long been my dad's favourite post-work nibble – accompanied with a beer, of course.

## Ingredients

80–100 g (2¾–3½ oz) Bombay mix (see Note)

¼ red onion, finely diced

juice of ¼ lemon

10–15 g (¼–½ oz) coriander (cilantro), leaves and stems finely chopped

Morning Masala Chai (page 49) or beer, to serve

## Method

Add all of the ingredients to a small bowl and stir thoroughly.

Serve with a mug of chai or a cold beer.

**Note**

My favourite Bombay mix is made by Cofresh. Look for it in Indian supermarkets or online.

# Masala Eggy Bread

Serves 2

A savoury variant on the classic French toast with a spicy twist. This is one to be enjoyed on a Sunday morning (or any morning you're not in a rush to get out) and is best served with fresh tomatoes and avocado.

## Ingredients

2 tablespoons milk or plant-based milk
3 eggs
2 garlic cloves, minced
1 green chilli, finely chopped, to taste
10–15 g (¼–½ oz) coriander (cilantro), leaves and stems finely chopped
4 slices sourdough or your bread of choice
30 g (1 oz) salted butter or vegan butter
1 teaspoon olive oil

**Spice Blend**

¼ teaspoon ground turmeric
½ teaspoon ground red chilli
½–1 teaspoon salt, to taste

**To Serve**

sliced cherry tomatoes
sliced avocado
olive oil
tomato ketchup (optional)

## Method

Whisk the milk and eggs together in a large shallow bowl until well combined.

Add the garlic, chilli, coriander and the spice blend and whisk again.

Place two slices of bread in the bowl at a time, letting them soak for a few seconds before turning them over – both sides of the bread should be well coated in the egg batter.

Heat the butter and olive oil in a large frying pan over medium heat until the butter starts to sizzle.

Add two slices of the egg-coated bread and cook for 3–4 minutes on each side until golden brown all over. Repeat with the remaining slices of bread.

Serve topped with tomato and avocado and a drizzle of olive oil. Add a sprinkle of salt and pepper or a generous squeeze of ketchup.

# Inda Kanda nu Shaak

(Scrambled Egg & Onion)

Serves 2

This quick, fuss-free recipe works just as well for lunch as it does for dinner. I prefer to use red onion, cooking it very briefly so that it keeps its crunch. Serve on toasted sourdough with some slices of avocado or, my favourite, a drizzle of tomato ketchup.

## Ingredients

4 eggs

50 ml (1¾ fl oz) milk or plant-based milk

1 green chilli, finely chopped, to taste

2 tablespoons olive oil, salted butter or vegan butter

1 small red onion, sliced

**Spice Blend**

½ teaspoon ground coriander

½ teaspoon ground cumin

¼ teaspoon ground turmeric

¼ teaspoon ground red chilli

½ teaspoon garlic granules

½–1 teaspoon salt, to taste

**To Serve**

finely chopped coriander (cilantro), leaves and stems

toasted sourdough slices, buttered

sliced avocado (optional)

tomato ketchup (optional)

## Method

Whisk the eggs, milk, chilli and spice blend together in a bowl, then set aside.

Heat the olive oil in a large frying pan over medium heat. Add the onion and cook, stirring, for 4–5 minutes, until it starts to colour slightly. You want the onion to still have a slight crunch, so don't overcook it.

Add the egg mixture and reduce the heat to low. Using a spatula, fold the egg in a figure-of-eight motion for 3–4 minutes, or until the egg is cooked to your liking.

Scatter some coriander on top of the scrambled egg and serve on buttered toast with slices of avocado or a drizzle of ketchup, if desired.

# Vaghaar Baked Beans on Toast

Serves 2–3

I've always loved the simplicity of beans on toast, a timeless comfort that works for breakfast, lunch or dinner. Here they are embellished with a touch of Indian spice. For something heartier, try them over a buttered baked potato topped with a sprinkle of cheese.

## Ingredients

½ white onion, diced

2–3 garlic cloves, minced

1 green chilli, finely chopped, to taste

415 g (14½ oz) tinned baked beans

1 teaspoon tomato paste (concentrated puree)

toasted sourdough slices or baked potatoes, to serve

butter and cheddar cheese, to serve

**Vaghaar**

1 tablespoon olive oil

½ teaspoon cumin seeds

½ teaspoon carom (ajwain) seeds

**Spice Blend**

½ teaspoon ground coriander

½ teaspoon ground cumin

¼ teaspoon ground turmeric

½ teaspoon ground red chilli

½ teaspoon salt, to taste

## Method

For the vaghaar, heat the olive oil in a saucepan over medium heat. Add the cumin seeds and carom seeds and fry, giving the pan a swirl now and then, for 2 minutes, or until their aromas are released. As soon as you start to smell the spices, the vaghaar is ready – you don't want to burn the spices.

Stir in the onion, reduce the heat to low, cover and simmer for 8–10 minutes, or until the onion has softened and browned.

Stir in the garlic, chilli and spice blend and cook for 1–2 minutes. Stir in the beans and tomato paste and cook, stirring occasionally, for another 5 minutes, or until the beans are hot.

Serve on toast or on a baked potato topped with butter and a sprinkle of cheese.

# Crunchy Papri Chaat

Serves 6–8

This quintessential Indian street food is crunchy, packed with flavour and texture and works great as both a starter and a snack. Using a few store-bought elements, it can be thrown together in no time and it certainly won't fail to impress. Make sure to eat it the same day it's prepared, otherwise the crackers will turn soggy – although, given how popular it is at dinner parties, I don't think that will be an issue.

## Ingredients

- 100 g (3½ oz) plain or coconut-based yoghurt
- 1 tablespoon honey
- juice of ½ lemon
- 3 small all-purpose potatoes, peeled and cut into 1–1.5 cm (½ in) cubes
- 200 g (7 oz) chaat puri or crackers (see Notes)
- 1 red onion, diced
- 1 tomato, diced
- 200 g (7 oz) tinned chickpeas (garbanzo beans), drained and rinsed
- 4–5 tablespoons green chutney (store-bought or see page 234)
- 4–5 tablespoons tamarind chutney

**To Serve**

- sev (see Notes)
- pomegranate seeds
- chaat masala (optional)
- finely chopped coriander (cilantro), leaves and stems

## Method

Whisk the yoghurt, honey and lemon juice together in a small bowl with 1 tablespoon of water. Set aside.

Put the potato in a saucepan and add enough water to cover. Bring to the boil over medium–high heat, then cook for 8–10 minutes, or until the potato is easily pierced with a knife. Drain and set aside until completely cool.

Cover the bottom of a deep serving dish with a layer of chaat puri. Next, evenly distribute the potato, onion, tomato and chickpeas over the chaat puri. Drizzle the yoghurt mixture and both chutneys evenly on top of the vegetables.

To serve, top with a generous layer of sev, pomegranate seeds, a sprinkle of chaat masala, if using, and a scattering of coriander.

Enjoy straight away.

**Notes**

I like the Jaimin brand chaat puri. If you can't find an Indian-style cracker, plain crackers will do the trick.

I prefer the Cofresh brand of sev, but any brand will do.

# Small Plates

*Nani Thali*

The recipes in this chapter show the influence Western cuisine has had on Mum's cooking, from her Indian twists on classic dishes to experimentation with Indo-Chinese flavours. When our extended family get together, my mum often picks three-to-five small plates to serve up as a tapas-style spread. The mixed veg bhajis and samosas are my favourites – those who know me know I love a fried treat! That said, all of these plates are as delicious as they are nostalgic for me, and I'd encourage you to try cooking something new.

These recipes vary in terms of time investment. A quick plate can be prepped in twenty minutes, usually the ones that are made in a single tray or pan, while others require a bit more dedication or even an extra pair of hands. So, whether you're hoping to impress friends at a dinner party or someone's just popped in for a catch-up, this chapter can meet your needs from breakfast time right through to the evening.

CORNFLOUR
GLUTEN FREE

# Baked Handvo

(Savoury Veg Cake)

Serves 8–10

Surprisingly, cake doesn't always have to be sweet. Although this includes an overnight step, don't let that scare you off. This savoury 'cake' requires a lot less technical precision than baking. It's one of my aunt Rash Foi's signature dishes. She taught me that you can pack it with any vegetables you like, making it a great way to use up leftovers and avoid food waste. For a softer, spongier texture, simply add a little extra yoghurt.

## Ingredients

150 g (5½ oz) ondhwa flour (see Notes)

50 g (1¾ oz) coarse semolina

25 g (1 oz) gram (besan) flour

½ teaspoon ground turmeric

1½ teaspoons salt

400 g (14 oz) plain or coconut-based yoghurt (see Notes)

8–10 garlic cloves, minced

5–6 green chillies, finely chopped, to taste

2 carrots, grated

2 small courgettes (zucchini), grated

½ large dudhi (bottle gourd) or courgette, grated

1 white onion, roughly diced

100 g (⅔ cup) frozen peas

100 g (⅔ cup) frozen sweetcorn

¼ teaspoon citric acid

¼ teaspoon Eno or baking powder (see Notes)

juice of ½ lemon

Tomato Chutney (page 233), to serve

**Vaghaar**

2–3 tablespoons sunflower or vegetable oil

1 teaspoon black mustard seeds

1 teaspoon white sesame seeds, plus extra for sprinkling

## Method

**Day 1**

Combine the ondhwa flour, semolina, gram flour, turmeric and salt in a large mixing bowl. Stir in the yoghurt until combined. The mixture will be slightly runny in consistency. Cover and set aside to rest at room temperature overnight (or at least 8 hours).

**Day 2**

The following day, the fermented mixture should have a thick, slightly stiff consistency.

Stir the garlic, chilli, carrot, courgette, dudhi, onion, peas and sweetcorn into the yoghurt mixture. The mixture should now be predominantly vegetables. If not, add a bit more veg.

Combine the citric acid, Eno and lemon juice in a small bowl, then stir it into the mixture. Set aside.

Preheat the oven to 180°C (350°F) and line a 25 × 35 cm (10 × 12 in) baking tray, 5–6 cm (2–2½ in) deep, with baking paper.

Transfer the handvo mixture to the baking tray.

For the vaghaar, heat the oil in a saucepan over medium heat. Add the mustard seeds and sesame seeds and fry, giving the pan a swirl now and then, for 2 minutes, or until the mustard seeds start to pop and sizzle. Immediately take the pan off the heat.

Pour the vaghaar over the handvo mixture in the baking tray, making sure the seeds are evenly spread across the top – you can use the back of a spoon to spread them if needed. Sprinkle an extra pinch of sesame seeds over the top.

Place the tray in the oven and bake for 40 minutes, or until a crispy golden brown layer has formed on top of the cake.

Cut into squares in the tray and serve with tomato chutney. You can serve the cake hot or cold, though I prefer it hot.

**Notes**

Ondhwa flour is a mix of chana daal (yellow gram lentils) and rice flour. I prefer the Jalpur brand ondhwa flour. Look for it in Indian supermarkets or online.

If using coconut-based yoghurt, you will find the consistency will be runny after fermentation. Therefore, make sure to pack the mixture with more grated veg. Also add in an extra ½ teaspoon of citric acid and the juice of a whole lemon instead of ½ lemon. Because coconut-based yoghurt doesn't ferment, it's harder to achieve the same sour taste as plain yoghurt.

Eno makes the texture of the cake fluffier and lighter and is preferred, but if you can't get it, baking powder still works fine.

SPECIAL OFFER
£ 4.99 kg

# Fluffy Dhokla (Steamed Savoury Cake)

Serves 4–6

This is a comforting, anytime savoury treat. In our family we usually whip this up when we're expecting guests. It is best served warm with sev, tamarind and *Fresh Green Chutney*. The light, fluffy body of the cake gives a nice contrasting breadth of textures when paired with the crunchy and wet toppings.

## Ingredients

250 g (9 oz) dhokla flour (see Notes)

3 heaped tablespoons plain yoghurt

120 ml (4 fl oz) warm water

4–5 green chillies, finely chopped, to taste

2–3 cm (¾–1¼ in) piece of ginger, grated

¼ teaspoon citric acid or 1 tablespoon lemon juice

1 teaspoon Eno or baking powder (see Notes)

**Spice Blend**

¼ teaspoon ground turmeric

1½ teaspoons salt

½ teaspoon sugar

**Vaghaar**

2 tablespoons sunflower or vegetable oil

1 teaspoon black mustard seeds

1 teaspoon white sesame seeds

**To Serve**

Fresh Green Chutney (page 234)

tamarind chutney thinned with a little boiling water

sev (see Notes)

finely chopped coriander (cilantro), leaves and stems

## Method

Sift the dhokla flour into a large mixing bowl.

Add the yoghurt, then slowly pour in the warm water while whisking to create a smooth batter. The batter should slowly but easily slide off a spoon. Add more water if needed.

Add the chilli, ginger and spice blend and whisk to combine. Cover and set aside to rest at room temperature for at least 10 minutes.

Next, whisk in the citric acid and Eno until the mixture becomes foamy and you start to see air bubbles. This is important as it ensures the dhokla will be light and fluffy. The consistency should still be the same.

Spread a thin layer of sunflower or vegetable oil into an 18–20 cm (7–8 in) round, 4–5 cm (1½–2 in) deep, metal tray. Make sure the tray will fit into the saucepan you'll use to steam the dhokla.

Transfer the dhokla mixture to the tray and smooth the top.

Fill a large saucepan with 2–3 cm (¾–1¼ in) of water, place a steamer basket inside and bring the water to the boil over medium–high heat. Carefully place the metal tray on top of the basket. Tie a tea towel around the steamer basket lid before covering the pan – this will ensure the tea towel absorbs any excess water. Steam for 25–30 minutes.

At the end of cooking, remove the tray from the pan and set aside while you make the vaghaar.

Heat the oil in a saucepan over medium heat. Add the mustard seeds and sesame seeds and fry, giving the pan a swirl now and then, for 2 minutes, or until the mustard seeds start to pop and sizzle. Immediately take the pan off the heat.

Pour the vaghaar over the dhokla, making sure the seeds are evenly spread across the top – you can use the back of spoon to spread them if needed.

To serve, cut the dhokla into slices and serve hot with a drizzle of each of the chutneys, a sprinkle of sev and some coriander.

The dhokla will keep refrigerated for up to 3 days. Reheat in the microwave to revive the moist texture.

### Notes

Dhokla flour is a mix of gram (besan) flour and coarse semolina. If you can't find dhokla flour (I prefer Jalpur brand) in an Indian grocery store, mix 200 g (7 oz) of gram flour and 50 g (1¾ oz) of coarse semolina.

Eno makes the texture of the cake fluffier and lighter and is preferred, but if you can't find it, baking powder still works fine.

I prefer the Cofresh brand of sev, but any brand will do.

# Mixed Veg Bhajis

Serves 8–10 *(Makes 20)*

Making a delicious Indian fried treat often means a little kitchen mess and veg bhajis are no exception – expect a few splashes of batter and oil across your surfaces. They are best enjoyed hot and crispy, dipped in *Tomato Chutney* and/or *Fresh Green Chutney*. Feel free to swap in your favourite vegetables and see how they taste in the spicy batter.

## Ingredients

200 g (7 oz) gram (besan) flour

½ teaspoon baking powder

10–15 g (¼–½ oz) coriander (cilantro), leaves and stems finely chopped

4–5 green chillies, finely chopped, to taste

juice of 1 lemon

150 ml (5 fl oz) cold water (see Notes)

2 large white onions, halved, then sliced into 5 mm (¼ in) semi-circles

1 large white all-purpose potato, sliced into 5 mm (¼ in) rounds

1 large aubergine (eggplant), sliced into 5 mm (¼ in) rounds

sunflower or vegetable oil, for deep-frying

**Spice Blend**

½ teaspoon ground turmeric

1 tablespoon cumin seeds

1 tablespoon ground cumin

1 teaspoon ground red chilli

2–3 teaspoons salt, to taste

**To Serve**

salt

lemon wedges

Tomato Chutney (page 233) and/or Fresh Green Chutney (page 234)

## Method

Whisk the gram flour, baking powder, coriander, chilli and spice blend together in a large mixing bowl. Add the lemon juice and cold water and stir until you've created a sticky consistency. Make sure the batter isn't too runny as it needs to stick to the veg. Add more flour if needed.

Transfer a third of the batter to a separate bowl and add the onion slices, mixing until they are completely covered in the batter. This step is easiest to do with your hands.

Mix the potato and aubergine slices through the remaining batter, ensuring the slices are completely covered.

Heat the oil in a large deep saucepan over medium heat. To check the oil is hot enough, drop a little batter into the oil – if it sizzles and browns quickly it's hot enough. (Alternatively, the oil should reach 180°C/350°F on a cooking thermometer.)

For the onion bhajis, press the mixture together into balls, then flatten until they are roughly 5–6 cm (2–2½ in) in diameter – the thinner the better.

Carefully lower three or four bhajis (I always cook the onion bhajis first and then the aubergine and potato bhajis) into the pan using a slotted spoon or tongs. (How many you can fit in the pan will depend on the size of your pan.) Reduce the heat to medium–low and fry the bhajis for 6–7 minutes on each side, until golden brown. While the bhajis are cooking, prepare a plate lined with paper towel to absorb any excess oil. Remove each cooked bhaji with tongs and transfer it to the paper towel. Continue until all the bhajis are cooked.

Sprinkle the bhajis with salt and serve hot with lemon wedges and one or two bowls of chutney on the side for dipping.

### Notes

If you'd like to make beer-battered bhajis, use only 75 ml (2½ fl oz) of cold water and add 75 ml (2½ fl oz) of cold lager. The lager makes the batter crispier.

If you have one, use a mandoline to slice the vegetables into thin rounds – you don't want the slices to be too thick as they won't cook in the oil.

Try mixing up the vegetables by using grated carrot, sweet potato, courgette (zucchini) and finely chopped cabbage.

# Sticky Cauliflower

Serves 4 *(As a side dish)*

This isn't a traditional Gujarati dish and leans more towards Indo-Chinese flavours. The marinade is a favourite in our household and it makes a great vegan option if you're putting on a bigger spread. Make sure to cook your onions and bell peppers on a high heat to create that slightly charred, smoky finish.

This is a great dish to serve alongside *Matar Paneer* (page 139) or *Buttery Jeera Chicken* (page 107).

## Ingredients

1 large cauliflower, florets only
2–3 tablespoons sesame oil
1 red onion, thinly sliced
1 red bell pepper (capsicum), thinly sliced

**Marinade**

1 tablespoon sesame oil
2 tablespoons soy sauce
1 tablespoon honey
1 tablespoon tomato ketchup
3–4 garlic cloves, minced
2–3 cm (¾–1¼ in) piece of ginger, grated
2 green chillies, finely chopped, to taste
1 tablespoon paprika
1 teaspoon all-spice
1 teaspoon ground black pepper
2 teaspoons salt, to taste

**To Serve**

½ lemon
chopped spring onions (scallions)
white sesame seeds

## Method

Put the cauliflower florets and a sprinkle of salt in a saucepan and add enough water to cover. Bring the water to the boil over medium–high heat and cook the cauliflower for 6–8 minutes, until slightly tender. Drain.

Whisk the marinade ingredients together in a large bowl.

Add the cauliflower florets to the marinade and stir until they are evenly coated. Cover and place in the fridge to marinate for at least 3 hours, but overnight will give the best results.

Heat the sesame oil in a large frying pan over high heat. Add the onion and bell pepper and fry, tossing intermittently, for 4–5 minutes, or until slightly charred. Don't overcook the vegetables – you want them to still have a crunch. (However, if you'd prefer softer onions and bell peppers, cook them for longer over a lower heat.)

Reduce the heat to medium and add the marinated cauliflower florets and 60–80 ml (¼–⅓ cup) of water. Toss to combine and cook the vegetables for 8–10 minutes, stirring once or twice, until the cauliflower is heated through and starting to brown slightly.

To serve, squeeze the lemon half over the cauliflower mixture and sprinkle with the spring onion and sesame seeds.

# Masala Shakshuka

Serves 2–3

This Gujarati twist on the Middle Eastern shakshuka is a perfect brunch option, especially with some quality sourdough to mop up the spicy tomatoey sauce. The eggs are traditionally poached, but feel free to substitute your favourite type of eggs – fried, boiled or scrambled.

## Ingredients

2 tablespoons olive oil
1 white onion, diced
3 tomatoes, diced
6 garlic cloves, minced
3–4 cm (1¼–1½ in) piece of ginger, grated
2 green chillies, finely chopped, to taste
1 tablespoon tomato paste (concentrated puree)
2 tablespoons double (heavy) cream or vegan cream (optional)
200 g (7 oz) baby spinach, roughly chopped
4 eggs
½ lemon
10–15 g (¼–½ oz) coriander (cilantro), leaves and stems finely chopped
sourdough, to serve

**Spice Blend**

1 heaped teaspoon ground coriander
1 heaped teaspoon ground cumin
1 teaspoon ground turmeric
½ teaspoon garam masala
1 teaspoon ground red chilli
1 teaspoon salt, to taste

## Method

Heat the olive oil in a large frying pan over medium heat. Stir in the onion, reduce the heat to low and cover with a lid. Simmer for 8–10 minutes, until the onion has softened and browned. Stir in the tomato, garlic, ginger, chilli, tomato paste and spice blend. Cover and simmer for 12–15 minutes, until the tomato has softened.

Add the cream, if using, spinach and 120 ml (4 fl oz) of water and stir for 2–3 minutes, until the spinach starts to wilt.

Using a spoon, make four wells in the sauce and crack an egg into each of them. Cover the pan and simmer the eggs for 6–8 minutes, until the whites are cooked but the yolks are still runny.

Remove from the heat, squeeze the lemon half over the top and scatter with the coriander.

Place the frying pan on a heatproof mat in the centre of your table and serve directly from the pan with slices of sourdough bread. This dish goes well with a glass of orange juice.

# Sweet Chilli Paneer

Serves 3–4

Although you can make paneer in the classic tomato sauce that many of the vegetarian recipes in this book use, my mum likes to mix it up with a sweet chilli tang. This is a vibrant, colourful dish that always goes down well with vegetarians.

## Ingredients

3 tablespoons olive oil

225 g (8 oz) paneer, cut into 2–3 cm (¾–1¼ in) cubes

1 white onion, sliced

1 red bell pepper (capsicum), sliced

3–4 garlic cloves, minced

2–3 cm (¾–1¼ in) piece of ginger, grated

1 green chilli, finely chopped, to taste

3 tablespoons sweet chilli sauce

**Spice Blend**

½ teaspoon ground red chilli

1 teaspoon salt, to taste

## Method

Heat 1 tablespoon of the olive oil in a large frying pan over medium heat. Add the paneer cubes and fry on each side for 3–4 minutes, until golden brown and crispy.

Add the remaining 2 tablespoons of olive oil to the pan, along with the onion, bell pepper, garlic, ginger, chilli and spice blend and stir to combine. Cook, stirring occasionally, for 6–8 minutes, until the onion and bell pepper are slightly charred.

Stir in the sweet chilli sauce and cook for a further 2–3 minutes.

Serve on its own as a starter.

# Spicy Pea Pastries

Serves 6 *(Makes 10–12)*

This is a twist on the classic pea kachori, the perfect bite-sized snack for when guests come over. This recipe is truly simple, pairing spiced, nutritious peas with flaky puff pastry (to be honest, anything wrapped in pastry is a winner for me). Not a fan of peas? Swap them out for courgette (zucchini), potato or aubergine (eggplant) instead and cook the filling for longer.

## Ingredients

250 g (9 oz) frozen peas
4–5 garlic cloves, chopped
2–3 cm (¾–1¼ in) piece of ginger, chopped
1 green chilli, chopped, to taste
1 white onion, diced
juice of ½ lemon
10–15 g (¼–½ oz) coriander (cilantro), leaves and stems finely chopped
23 × 35 cm (9 × 13¾ in) store-bought puff pastry sheet
20 ml (¾ fl oz) milk or oat milk
Tomato Chutney (page 233), to serve

**Vaghaar**

2 tablespoons olive oil
1 teaspoon black mustard seeds
1 teaspoon cumin seeds

**Spice Blend**

1 heaped teaspoon ground coriander
1 heaped teaspoon ground cumin
¼ teaspoon ground turmeric
½ teaspoon ground cinnamon
1 teaspoon ground red chilli
1–2 teaspoons salt, to taste

## Method

Pulse the peas, garlic, ginger and chilli in a food processor until coarse – you don't want to mash the peas. Set aside.

For the vaghaar, heat the olive oil in a saucepan over medium heat. Add the mustard seeds and cumin seeds and fry, giving the pan a swirl now and then, for 2 minutes, or until the mustard seeds start to pop and sizzle.

Stir in the onion, and cook for 3–4 minutes. Stir in the pea mixture and spice blend. Simmer for 6–8 minutes, until the peas have defrosted.

Remove from the heat and stir through the lemon juice and coriander. Set the filling aside to cool.

Preheat the oven to 200°C (400°F) and line a baking tray with baking paper.

Lay the pastry sheet flat on a surface. Add the cooled filling in a line along one long edge of the sheet. Fold the sheet over tightly, creating a long cylindrical shape, then continue to roll it over until you reach the other end. Use a sharp knife to cut 4–5 cm (1½–2 in) thick slices. Place the rolls on the baking tray, cut side up, and brush the exposed pastry with milk.

Bake for 25–30 minutes, rotating the tray halfway through cooking, until the pastry is puffed and golden.

Serve hot with a bowl of tomato chutney for dipping.

# Kobi na Motiya (Cabbage Kofta)

Serves 6–8 *(Makes 20–25)*

Cabbage is often underrated, but these vegetable-packed koftas show just how tasty it can be. When shaping the mixture, you can go for the classic kofta shape or a flatter fritter – both are equally delicious. Enjoy them as a snack on their own, dipped into *Mint Yoghurt* or as a patty in an Indian-style burger for something a little different.

## Ingredients

½ white cabbage

1 carrot

150 g (5½ oz) curly kale

150 g (5½ oz) gram (besan) flour

30 g (1 oz) plain (all-purpose) flour (see Note)

1–2 garlic cloves, minced

3 cm (1¼ in) piece of ginger, grated

3 green chillies, finely chopped, to taste

10–15 g (¼–½ oz) coriander (cilantro), leaves and stems finely chopped

juice of ½ lemon

60 ml (¼ cup) olive oil

Mint Yoghurt (page 231), to serve

**Spice Blend**

1 heaped teaspoon ground coriander

1 heaped teaspoon ground cumin

½ teaspoon ground turmeric

½ teaspoon garam masala

½ teaspoon ground red chilli

1 teaspoon sugar

1 teaspoon salt, to taste

## Method

Blitz the cabbage, carrot and kale in a food processor until finely minced. Alternatively, you can grate or finely chop the vegetables.

Transfer the vegetables to a large mixing bowl, add both flours, the garlic, ginger, chilli, coriander and spice blend and use your hands to combine well. Stir in the lemon juice and add 50 ml (1¾ fl oz) of cold water if the mixture feels dry. If the vegetable mixture is still coarse and doesn't bind together in your hands, use a hand-held blender to blitz the mixture further.

Place a large heatproof plate in the oven and preheat the oven to 140°C (285°F).

Roll small handfuls of the mixture into oblong-shaped koftas and place them on a large tray or plate.

Heat the olive oil in a large frying pan over medium heat. Carefully add around ten koftas to the pan. (How many you can fit in the pan will depend on the size of your pan.) Reduce the heat to medium–low and fry the koftas for 8–10 minutes on each side, until crispy and golden brown. Transfer them to the oven to keep warm, then continue frying the koftas until they are all cooked.

Serve the koftas warm with mint yoghurt.

**Note**

Substitute plain flour for gluten-free flour or add more gram flour to make these koftas gluten free.

# Texts From Home
## Kobi na Motiya

Heat some oil in a pan to shallow-fry the motiyas,
bind small handfuls and put in the hot oil.
Keep on low-medium heat,
turn over once browned on one side.
Not sure of timing,
maybe look at after 8–10 minutes each side.

*Rash Foi*

# Crispy Patra

*(Taro Leaf Rolls)*

Serves 4–6 *(Makes about 30)*

Taro leaves are packed with nutrients, rich in vitamins, minerals and antioxidants. Patra rolls can be enjoyed either steamed or fried – although I prefer the fried version. At home, Dad and I often fight over the leftover sweet-and-sour crispy onions and golden scraps from the pan.

## Ingredients

130–150 g (4½ –5½ oz) patra (taro) leaves (see Notes)

2 tablespoons olive oil

1 teaspoon black mustard seeds

1 white onion, diced

½ lemon, to serve

sugar, to serve

**Chickpea Paste**

150 g (5½ oz) gram (besan) flour

30 g (1 oz) rice flour

1 tablespoon tamarind sauce or puree

260 ml (9 fl oz) warm water

2 teaspoons goor (jaggery) mixed with 50 ml (1¾ fl oz) boiling water to make a paste (see Notes)

2 teaspoons olive oil

3–4 garlic cloves, minced

2–3 cm (¾–1¼ in) piece of ginger, grated

5–6 green chillies, finely chopped, to taste

1 teaspoon ground coriander

1 teaspoon ground cumin

¼ teaspoon ground turmeric

1 teaspoon ground red chilli

1 teaspoon salt, to taste

¼ teaspoon baking powder

## Method

Prepare the patra (taro) leaves by cutting out the thick middle stalks, being careful not to tear the leaves. This will ensure that the leaves roll tightly together. Wash the leaves thoroughly and let them soak in cold water for 5–10 minutes. Pat the leaves dry and carefully wrap them in a dry tea towel.

Make the chickpea paste by whisking the two flours, tamarind sauce and warm water together in a large bowl until you have a sticky, paste-like consistency. Add the goor paste, olive oil, garlic, ginger, chilli, spices, salt and baking powder and stir to combine.

Place a large taro leaf on your work surface with the underside of the leaf facing up. Spread a generous layer of chickpea paste over the leaf using your fingers. Place a similar sized or slightly smaller leaf on top, front side down, and add another coating of chickpea paste. (You can add more leaf layers depending on the desired thickness of the roll.)

Next, fold both long sides of the leaf stack inwards, then tightly roll the leaves up from the bottom, creating a cylinder. Set aside and repeat until you have used up all the leaves.

Fill a saucepan with 2–3 cm (¾–1¼ in) of water, place a steamer on top and bring the water to the boil over medium heat. Add the taro leaf rolls in a single layer to the steamer. (If they don't all fit, steam them in two batches.)

Steam for 15–18 minutes, or until you can poke a knife through the centre of a roll and it comes out clean. Remove the rolls from the steamer and set aside to cool slightly before slicing into 1.5–2 cm (½–¾ in) discs.

Heat the olive oil in a large frying pan over medium heat. Add the mustard seeds and cook for 2 minutes, or until they start to pop and sizzle. Add the onion, increase the heat to high, and cook, tossing intermittently, for 4–5 minutes, until crisp. Reduce the heat slightly, place the patra discs in the pan and fry for 6–8 minutes on each side, or until crispy and browned.

Transfer the patra to a platter and serve them hot with a squeeze of lemon juice and a sprinkle of sugar.

**Notes**

You can use spring collard leaves or extra-large spinach leaves if you can't find taro leaves. Alternatively, use a mixture of taro and spinach leaves.

You can substitute brown sugar for the goor. There's no need to add boiling water to the brown sugar – just use it as is.

If you like, you can skip the frying step and serve the patra steamed, with a drizzle of olive oil; however, I love to crisp them up.

# Veg Samosa Filling

Serves 6–8 *(Makes 16–18)*

A guaranteed crowd-pleaser, this starter requires a fair bit of time in the kitchen but is undoubtedly worth the effort. Gujarati samosas are smaller than what you might find at your local Indian eatery, made with a thinner pastry and filled with a mixture of vegetables.

At Lad family get-togethers, a small team gathers around the table to assist with constructing the samosas, accompanied by lots of natter. This dish is both a great starter for special occasions and an opportunity to get your loved ones involved in the process. See page 98 for instructions for the pastry, assembly and cooking.

## Ingredients

1 large all-purpose potato, peeled and cut into 1 cm (½ in) cubes

380–400 g (13½–14 oz) diced frozen mixed vegetables (see Note)

2–3 garlic cloves, minced

2–3 cm (¾–1¼ in) piece of ginger, grated

2 green chillies, finely chopped, to taste

1 white onion, diced

10–15 g (¼–½ oz) coriander (cilantro), leaves and stems roughly chopped

**Vaghaar**

3 tablespoons olive oil

1 teaspoon black mustard seeds

1 teaspoon cumin seeds

**Spice Blend**

1 heaped teaspoon ground coriander

1 heaped teaspoon ground cumin

¼ teaspoon ground turmeric

1 teaspoon ground red chilli

1–2 teaspoons salt, to taste

## Method

For the vaghaar, heat the olive oil in a large saucepan over medium heat. Add the mustard seeds and cumin seeds and cook for 1–2 minutes, until the mustard seeds start to pop and sizzle.

Add the potato, frozen vegetables, garlic, ginger, chilli and spice blend, stirring well to combine. Cover and reduce the heat to low. Simmer for 15 minutes, or until the potato is soft, stirring occasionally and adding a splash of water if needed.

Remove the pan from the heat and stir in the onion and coriander – you don't want the onion to cook; this will happen when you fry the samosas. Transfer the samosa filling to a large bowl and set aside to cool.

**Note**

You can use any diced fresh or frozen vegetables – get creative – though the potato is a must!

# Lamb Samosa Filling

Serves 6–8 *(Makes 16–18)*

Lamb samosas are less common than the vegetarian variety, especially in Gujarati cuisine, but there are plenty of big meat eaters in my family for whom these are much more sought after.

These snacks really do fit any occasion and are super convenient for taking out when you're on the go. Personally, I like them best when they're freshly cooked and still warm, as that's when they're most crispy. See page 98 for instructions for the pastry, assembly and cooking.

## Ingredients

400–500 g (14 oz–1 lb 2 oz) minced (ground) lamb

4 garlic cloves, minced

2–3 cm (¾–1¼ in) piece of ginger, grated

2 green chillies, finely chopped, to taste

250 g (9 oz) frozen peas

1 white onion, diced

½ teaspoon garam masala

10–15 g (¼–½ oz) coriander (cilantro), leaves and stems roughly chopped

juice of ½ lemon

**Vaghaar**

2 tablespoons olive oil

3 whole cloves

2–3 small cinnamon sticks

**Spice Blend**

1 heaped teaspoon ground coriander

1 heaped teaspoon ground cumin

1 teaspoon ground turmeric

1½ teaspoons ground red chilli

2 teaspoons salt, to taste

## Method

For the vaghaar, heat the olive oil in a large saucepan over medium heat. Add the cloves and cinnamon sticks and cook for 2–3 minutes, until they start to release their aromas.

Add the minced lamb, garlic, ginger, chilli and spice blend, stirring well to break up the lamb thoroughly with a wooden spoon. Cover and reduce the heat to medium–low. Simmer for 15 minutes, stirring occasionally, until the lamb is browned and cooked through.

Remove the pan from the heat and stir in the peas, onion, garam masala, coriander and lemon juice – you don't want the onion to cook; this will happen when you fry the samosas. Transfer the samosa filling to a large bowl and set aside to cool.

# Samosa Pastry, Assembly & Cooking

Serves 6–8 *(Makes 20)*

Homemade pastry is truly the backbone of these samosas. While this is the most time-consuming part of the recipe, I highly recommend trying this out before reverting to store-bought pastry. If you want to make both vegetable and lamb samosas, double the quantity of this pastry recipe – and don't worry if that leaves you with too many, store them in the freezer to cook another time.

## Ingredients

375 g (2½ cups) plain (all-purpose) flour, plus more as required

1½ teaspoons ground cumin

1½ teaspoons cornflour (cornstarch)

1½ teaspoons olive oil, plus more as required

100 ml (3½ fl oz) boiling water

1 × Vegetable Samosa Filling (page 94) or Lamb Samosa Filling (page 95)

sunflower or vegetable oil, for deep-frying

Tomato Chutney (page 233) or tamarind chutney, to serve

## Method

Combine the flour, cumin and cornflour together in a large mixing bowl. Add the olive oil, then slowly pour the boiling water into the dry ingredients, using a wooden spoon to stir until you have a rough dough.

Turn the dough out onto your work surface and knead to bring it together. If the dough is too dry, add a little more water and a drizzle of oil. Keep kneading until you have a smooth dough.

Cover the dough with a tea towel and allow it to rest for 10 minutes.

After resting, divide the dough equally into ten pieces, then roll each piece into a small ball.

Set up one small bowl of olive oil (2 tablespoons) and another with plain flour (1 tablespoon). Lightly dust your work surface with flour.

Gently flatten each ball of dough, then use a rolling pin to roll the dough into 10 cm (4 in) circles, about 3 mm (⅛ in) thick.

Arrange the dough circles in pairs on your work surface. You will have five pairs. For each pair, brush the top of one circle with oil and dust the top of the other circle with flour. Place the floured circles, flour-side down, on top of the oiled circles – this will ensure the two circles don't stick together.

Heat a 25 cm (10 in) frying pan over medium–high heat.

Meanwhile, lightly dust your work surface with flour again. Roll the dough circles out again until they reach 20 cm (8 in) in diameter – they will be very thin.

Transfer a dough circle to the pan and cook it for 30 seconds, flip the circle over and cook for 30 seconds on the other side. Make sure the dough doesn't colour – you are not trying to cook the pastry. Remove the dough circle from the pan and immediately peel apart the two sheets – this needs to be done while the pastry is still hot.

Carefully wrap the hot pastry sheets stacked on top of each other in a clean tea towel to prevent them from drying out.

Repeat with the remaining dough and set aside until cool.

Slice the pastry circles in half to form semicircles. You will have 20 semicircles.

Combine 1 tablespoon of plain flour with 3 tablespoons of water in a small bowl to make a pastry glue.

Take a semicircle pastry sheet and fold the straight side in half to form a cone shape. Using your hand to support the cone, overlap the two straight edges and seal the sides together with pastry glue.

Hold the cone between your forefinger and thumb and fill it with 2–3 tablespoons of your chosen filling (picking out the cloves and cinnamon sticks if using the lamb filling).

Dab pastry glue along the outside open pastry edge, then fold the edges down into a box fold to fully enclose the filling. Make sure there are no gaps.

Repeat with the remaining pastry and filling to make 20 samosas.

Heat enough sunflower oil for deep-frying in a large deep saucepan over medium heat. To check the oil is hot enough, drop a little batter into the oil – if it sizzles and browns quickly it's hot enough. (Alternatively, the oil should reach 180°C/350°F on a cooking thermometer.)

Carefully lower three or four samosas into the pan using a slotted spoon or tongs. (How many you can fit in the pan will depend on the size of your pan.) Deep-fry for 3–4 minutes on each side, until golden brown. While the samosas are cooking, prepare a plate lined with paper towel to absorb any excess oil. Remove each cooked samosa with tongs and transfer it to the paper towel. Continue until all the samosas are cooked.

Serve the samosas with a bowl of tomato chutney or tamarind chutney for dipping.

**Note**

You can freeze uncooked samosas in an airtight container for up to 6 months. To cook from frozen, fry for 5–6 minutes on each side until golden.

# Sticky Chicken Wings

Serves 4–6

While I don't cook meat all that often, these Indo-Chinese sticky chicken wings are a real favourite of mine. My mum would always cook these for get-togethers and they're perfect with a simple salad as a starter. The straightforward marinade is tangy and sweet and, honestly, irresistibly tasty.

## Ingredients

1 kg (2 lb 3 oz) chicken wings

2 spring onions (scallions), chopped

10–15 g (¼–½ oz) coriander (cilantro), leaves and stems finely chopped

**Marinade**

1 tablespoon sesame oil

2 tablespoons soy sauce

1 tablespoon honey

1 tablespoon tomato ketchup

3–4 garlic cloves, minced

2 green chillies, finely chopped, to taste

1 tablespoon paprika

1 teaspoon all-spice

1 teaspoon ground black pepper

2 teaspoons salt, to taste

## Method

Combine the marinade ingredients together in a deep baking tray.

Add the chicken wings and toss until they are evenly coated in the marinade. Cover with foil and place in the fridge to marinate for at least 3 hours, but leave overnight for the best results.

Preheat the oven to 180°C (350°F).

Keep covered and bake the marinated chicken wings for 15 minutes. Remove the foil and give everything a stir. Add the spring onions and cook for another 15 minutes, uncovered.

Remove the tray from the oven, sprinkle the coriander over the chicken wings and stir. Serve hot and be sure to supply plenty of serviettes for sticky fingers.

**Note**

You can air-fry or barbecue the chicken wings for crispier skin or a charred taste. Cook for 20 minutes for both methods.

# Baked Chicken Spring Rolls

Serves 10–12 *(Makes 30–40)*

This is another venture into Indo-Chinese cuisine, combining spring roll pastry with an Indian spiced filling. I've always found these are a great side to bring to a dinner party – guests are always pleasantly surprised when they bite into one, expecting a classic Chinese spring roll but discovering an Indian twist.

## Ingredients

- 2 tablespoons sesame oil
- 350 g (12½ oz) minced (ground) or diced chicken (see Notes)
- 3–4 garlic cloves, minced
- 2–3 cm (¾–1¼ in) piece of ginger, grated
- 2 green chillies, finely chopped, to taste
- 150 g (1 cup) frozen peas
- 150 g (1 cup) frozen sweetcorn
- 1 tablespoon soy sauce
- 2–3 spring onions (scallions), chopped
- 1 red onion, diced
- 10–15 g (¼–½ oz) coriander (cilantro), leaves and stems finely chopped
- 40 × square 21.5 cm (8½ in) frozen spring roll pastry sheets
- sunflower or vegetable oil, for brushing
- sweet chilli sauce or tamarind dipping sauce, to serve

**Spice Blend**

- 1 heaped teaspoon ground coriander
- 1 heaped teaspoon ground cumin
- ¼ teaspoon ground turmeric
- ½ teaspoon ground red chilli
- 1–2 teaspoons salt, to taste

## Method

Heat the sesame oil in a large frying pan over medium heat. Add the minced chicken, garlic, ginger, chilli and spice blend, stirring until the minced chicken is evenly coated in the spices. Cook for around 8–10 minutes, stirring occasionally, until the minced chicken is browned and cooked through.

Stir in the peas, sweetcorn and soy sauce and cook for a further 3–4 minutes.

Remove the pan from the heat and stir in the spring onion, red onion and coriander – you don't want the onion to cook; this will happen when you fry the spring rolls. Transfer the filling to a large bowl and set aside to cool.

Preheat the oven to 180°C (350°F) and line one or two baking trays with baking paper. Fill a small bowl with cold water – this will be used as your pastry glue.

Lay a pastry sheet on your work surface. Add a heaped tablespoon of filling in a line along one edge of the sheet. Add a line of water on the other side of the sheet, then fold the sides inwards by around 2 cm (¾ in) to cover the ends of the filling. Roll the sheet up tightly to create a long cylindrical shape. Continue until you have used up all the filling and pastry sheets.

Place the spring rolls on the baking trays and brush them with sunflower oil.

Bake for 25–30 minutes, rotating the tray halfway through cooking, until golden brown.

Serve hot with a bowl of sweet chilli sauce or tamarind dipping sauce.

**Notes**

You can use vegan mince to make these spring rolls meat-free. I prefer Quorn brand vegan mince.

If you prefer, you can deep-fry or air-fry the spring rolls at 180°C (350°F). They will take around 5–6 minutes to cook.

You can freeze uncooked spring rolls in an airtight container for up to 6 months. To cook from frozen, fry for 6–8 minutes.

# Spicy Crumbs Chicken

Serves 6–8

This dish is definitely a family favourite, especially for my sister who prefers English cuisine. Think of these as spicy chicken nuggets. They make great finger food with a dipping sauce (my favourite combo is mayo with sweet chilli) or combine with salad leaves and cucumber in a wrap, pita bread or sandwich for an easy lunch.

## Ingredients

950 g (2 lb 2 oz) skinless, boneless chicken breasts or chicken breast strips

5–6 green chillies, finely chopped, to taste

½ teaspoon ground red chilli

2 teaspoons salt, to taste

1 egg

sunflower or vegetable oil, for shallow-frying

½ lemon

dipping sauce of your choice or pita bread, salad leaves and diced cucumber, to serve (optional)

**Crumb**

2 tablespoons dried breadcrumbs

2 slices white bread, blitzed in a food processor

1 teaspoon ground black pepper

1 tablespoon finely chopped mixed herbs

1 tablespoon plain (all-purpose) flour

## Method

Combine all the crumb ingredients in a shallow bowl. Line a large plate or tray with baking paper.

Cut the chicken into strips and trim the fat off. Wash the chicken and pat it dry with paper towel.

In a separate large bowl, whisk together the fresh chilli, ground chilli, salt and egg. Add the chicken strips and stir until evenly coated in the egg batter.

Next, dip each chicken strip into the breadcrumb mixture until evenly coated, then set aside on the prepared plate or tray.

Heat the oil in a large frying pan over medium heat. Using tongs, carefully add eight-to-ten chicken strips to the pan. (How many you can fit in the pan will depend on the size of your pan.) Fry for 5–6 minutes on each side, until golden brown and crispy. While the chicken strips are cooking, line a plate with paper towel. Remove each cooked chicken strip with tongs and transfer it to the paper towel. Continue until all the chicken strips are cooked. Squeeze the lemon half over the chicken.

Serve with your favourite dipping sauce or in a wrap or sandwich with salad leaves and cucumber.

**Note**

For a vegan alternative, substitute the chicken with 300–350 g (10½–12½ oz) firm tofu cut into 1.5 × 5 cm (½ × 2 in) sticks.

For a healthier alternative to frying, air-fry the chicken. Spray the crumbed chicken with a little oil spray and cook for 10–12 minutes, turning halfway through cooking.

# Buttery Jeera Chicken

Serves 4

The butter in this dish makes the chicken extra soft, tender and juicy. As someone who's dairy intolerant, I can confirm that dairy-free butter works just as well. Use a piece of bread to soak up the cumin-infused buttery goodness left in the pan or serving dish. Serve as a side with *Mint Yoghurt* or enjoy as the main event wrapped in *Yoghurt Naan Bread* with some *Versatile Salad*.

## Ingredients

500–600 g (1 lb 2 oz–1 lb 5 oz) skinless, boneless chicken breasts or thighs

45 g (1½ oz) salted butter or vegan butter

4–5 garlic cloves, minced

2–3 cm (¾–1¼ in) piece of ginger, grated

2 green chillies, finely chopped, to taste

2 tablespoons plain or coconut-based yoghurt (optional)

2–3 spring onions (scallions), chopped

10–15 g (¼–½ oz) coriander (cilantro), leaves and stems finely chopped

Yoghurt Naan Bread (page 198), Versatile Salad (page 118) and Mint Yoghurt (page 231), to serve (optional)

**Vaghaar**

2 tablespoons olive oil

3–4 whole cloves

2–3 cinnamon sticks

5–6 curry leaves

1 teaspoon cumin seeds

**Spice Blend**

1 heaped teaspoon ground coriander

2 teaspoons ground cumin

1 teaspoon ground turmeric

½ teaspoon garam masala

½ teaspoon ground red chilli

1–2 teaspoons salt, to taste

## Method

Cut the chicken into 4–5 cm (1½–2 in) pieces and trim the fat off. Wash the chicken and pat it dry with paper towel.

For the vaghaar, heat the olive oil in a large saucepan over medium heat. Add the cloves, cinnamon sticks, curry leaves and cumin seeds and fry, giving the pan a swirl now and then, for 2 minutes, or until their aromas are released and the cumin seeds start to sizzle.

Reduce the heat to low and add the butter. Let it melt slowly in the pan, then stir in the garlic, ginger, chilli and spice blend. Add the chicken and stir until it is thoroughly coated in the spices. Add the yoghurt now, if using, and the spring onion. Cover with a lid and simmer for 15 minutes.

Remove the pan from the heat and stir in the coriander. Remove the cloves and cinnamon sticks.

Serve on its own with mint yoghurt or wrapped in naan with salad and a dollop of mint yoghurt.

# Keema Scotch Eggs

Serves 6

If anyone knew how to cook with lamb it was my dada. This Indian twist on a British pub classic was one of Dada's signature dishes – a special treat, especially on Christmas Day.

## Ingredients

4 eggs

6 garlic cloves, minced

2–3 cm (¾–1¼ in) piece of ginger, grated

1½ green chillies, finely chopped, to taste

juice of ½ lemon

3 tablespoons olive oil

400–450 g (14 oz–1 lb) minced (ground) lamb

2 spring onions (scallions) or 1 white onion, diced

Tomato Chutney (page 233) or Mint Yoghurt (page 231), to serve

lager, to serve

**Spice Blend**

1 heaped teaspoon ground coriander

1 heaped teaspoon ground cumin

1 teaspoon ground turmeric

½ teaspoon garam masala

1 teaspoon ground red chilli

1–2 teaspoons salt, to taste

## Method

Fill a bowl with cold water and set aside. Place the eggs in a saucepan, cover with cold water and bring to the boil. Boil for 4–5 minutes, then transfer the eggs to the cold water. Once cool, peel the eggs and set aside.

Whisk the garlic, ginger, chilli, lemon juice, 1 tablespoon of the olive oil and the spice blend together in a large mixing bowl. Add the minced lamb and use your hands to massage the seasoning into the lamb. Stir in the spring onion.

Cut the eggs into quarters – this ensures the scotch eggs are not too large and the meat cooks evenly.

Take a handful of minced lamb and carefully mould it around a quartered egg piece. Use enough mixture to cover the egg in a 1 cm (½ in) thick coating of minced lamb. Repeat to coat all the egg quarters.

Heat the remaining olive oil in a large frying pan over medium heat. Add the Scotch eggs and cover with a lid. Cook for 5 minutes, then remove the lid and turn each egg over using tongs. Increase the heat to high and cook for a further 5 minutes, turning again halfway through to let the meat brown all over.

Serve hot with tomato chutney or mint yoghurt as an afternoon snack, with a cold lager to bring a little British pub atmosphere into your home.

**Note**

For a more classic Scotch egg, add an outer layer of breadcrumbs. Prepare three bowls: one with a handful of flour, one with two beaten eggs and another with a cup of dried breadcrumbs. Cover each egg quarter in the flour, then the beaten egg, then the breadcrumbs. Deep-fry in vegetable oil for 4–5 minutes.

# Keema Pita Breads

Serves 4

These make the perfect spicy packed lunch or picnic option that can be easily assembled outside of the kitchen and taste great cold. For a vegan alternative, try using blitzed mushrooms – when my mum made this for the family, it was so convincing that my grandparents couldn't tell the difference!

## Ingredients

450–500 g (1 lb–1 lb 2 oz) minced (ground) lamb (see Note overleaf)

4 garlic cloves, minced

2–3 cm (¾–1¼ in) piece of ginger, grated

2 green chillies, finely chopped, to taste

½ white onion, diced

2–3 spring onions (scallions), sliced

150 g (1 cup) frozen peas

½ teaspoon garam masala

10–15 g (¼–½ oz) coriander (cilantro), leaves and stems finely chopped

juice of ¼ lemon

**Vaghaar**

3 tablespoons olive oil

4 whole cloves

1–2 cinnamon sticks

2–3 cardamom pods

2 bay leaves

**Spice Blend**

1 heaped teaspoon ground coriander

1 heaped teaspoon ground cumin

½ teaspoon ground turmeric

½ teaspoon ground red chilli

1–2 teaspoons salt, to taste

**To Serve**

store-bought pita breads

Mint Yoghurt (page 231)

Pickled Onions (page 237)

mixed salad leaves

## Method

For the vaghaar, heat the olive oil in a large saucepan over medium heat. Add the cloves, cinnamon sticks, cardamom pods and bay leaves and fry, giving the pan a swirl now and then, for 2 minutes, or until their aromas are released. As soon as you start to smell the spices the vaghaar is ready – you don't want to burn the spices.

Add the minced lamb, garlic, ginger and chilli. Break up the lamb thoroughly with a wooden spoon. Stir in the spice blend and cover with a lid. Reduce the heat to medium–low and cook for 5 minutes, then remove the lid to allow the liquid from the lamb to evaporate. Cook for 5 minutes more, stirring occasionally, until the lamb is cooked and browned.

Stir in the onion, spring onion and peas and cook for another 2–3 minutes, until the peas have defrosted. You want the onion to be crunchy.

Remove the cloves, cinnamon sticks, cardamom pods and bay leaves from the pan, then stir in the garam masala and remove from the heat.

Add the coriander and lemon juice and stir to combine.

Serve the keema stuffed in pita bread with mint yoghurt, pickled onions and your favourite salad leaves.

**Note**

Swap out the lamb for mushrooms by blitzing 500 g (1 lb 2 oz) of chestnut mushrooms in a food processor.

Add onions only when keema is nearly cooked
or spring onions.
Just cook it until the lamb is cooked.
x

*Mum*

# Tray-Baked Lamb Chops

Serves 4–6

Lamb chops are a family favourite and my mum picked up this tray-baked method from a family friend long before I was born – later making it her own with spices and extra vegetables. This recipe couldn't be easier, and it will leave you with lamb chops that are juicy, tender and full of flavour.

## Ingredients

18–20 lamb rib chops
(cutlets; around 1.5 kg/3 lb 5 oz)

2 white onions, quartered

150 g (5½ oz) sugar snap peas

150 g (5½ oz) baby corn

Mint Yoghurt (page 231), to serve

**Marinade**

1 tablespoon Greek or coconut-based yoghurt

10–15 g (¼–½ oz) coriander (cilantro), leaves and stems finely chopped

4 garlic cloves, minced

2–3 cm (¾–1¼ in) piece of ginger, grated

3 green chillies, finely chopped

1 heaped teaspoon ground coriander

1 heaped teaspoon ground cumin

1 teaspoon ground turmeric

1 teaspoon ground cinnamon

1½ teaspoons ground red chilli

½ teaspoon garam masala

2 teaspoons salt, to taste

## Method

To make the marinade, combine the yoghurt, coriander, garlic, ginger, chilli, spices and salt in a deep baking tray. Add the lamb chops and toss until they are evenly coated in the marinade. Cover with foil and place in the fridge to marinate for at least 3 hours, but overnight for the best results.

Preheat the oven to 180°C (350°F).

Transfer the marinated lamb chops to the oven and bake for 30 minutes.

Remove the foil and add the onion, sugar snap peas and baby corn. Give everything a stir, then cover and cook for another 20–30 minutes, until the meat is tender.

Serve as a starter with a bowl of mint yoghurt for dipping.

# Motiyas

(Lamb Meatballs)

Serves 4–6 *(12–15 small balls)*

These lamb meatballs make a great standalone starter or side, especially when generously dipped into a refreshing *Mint Yoghurt*. If you'd like a saucy tomato-based meatball curry, I recommend following the method from *Dada's Lamb Curry* (page 170) and swap out the lamb for motiyas for a delicious bowl of comfort food.

## Ingredients

4 garlic cloves, minced
2–3 cm (¾–1¼ in) piece of ginger, grated
2 green chillies, finely chopped, to taste
juice of ½ lemon
1 tablespoon olive oil
500 g (1 lb 2 oz) minced (ground) lamb
1 white onion, diced

**Spice Blend**
1 heaped teaspoon ground coriander
1 heaped teaspoon ground cumin
1 teaspoon ground turmeric
½ teaspoon garam masala
1 teaspoon ground red chilli
1–2 teaspoons salt, to taste

**Vaghaar**
2 tablespoons olive oil
3–4 whole cloves
1 cinnamon stick

**To Serve**
finely chopped spring onions (scallions)
finely chopped coriander (cilantro), leaves and stems
Mint Yoghurt (page 231)

## Method

Whisk the garlic, ginger, chilli, lemon juice, olive oil and spice blend together in a large mixing bowl. Add the minced lamb and massage the seasoning into the lamb. This step is easiest to do with your hands. Finally, stir in the onion.

Roll the mixture into 12–15 small balls.

Prepare a plate lined with paper towel to absorb any excess oil.

For the vaghaar, heat the olive oil in a large frying pan over medium heat. Add the cloves and cinnamon stick and fry, giving the pan a swirl now and then, for 1–2 minutes, until the aromas are released.

Working in batches, add the meatballs to the pan and fry for 6–8 minutes on each side, until golden brown and slightly crispy. Remove the meatballs with tongs and transfer them to the paper towel. Continue until all the meatballs are cooked.

To serve, scatter the spring onion and coriander on top. The meatballs are lovely dipped in mint yoghurt.

# Versatile Salad

Serves 4–6

Our dinner table is never without a salad. The ingredients vary depending on what's in the fridge, so this recipe is really more of a guide to which vegetables (and fruit) you can throw together, drizzled with Dad's tangy dressing. I love how the crunch of raw vegetables contrasts with the softness of a curry, and how the sweetness of fruit can balance out any spice.

## Ingredients

60 g (2 oz) mixed salad leaves
1 carrot, grated
10 cm (4 in) long cucumber, grated
80 g (2¾ oz) sugar snap peas, halved
80 g (2¾ oz) baby corn, halved
100 g (3½ oz) radishes, thinly sliced
100 g (3½ oz) cherry tomatoes, quartered
½ avocado, cubed
handful of croutons (optional)
½ apple, ½ pear or ¼ mango, cubed (optional)

**Dressing**
1 tablespoon olive oil
1½ teaspoons white wine vinegar
juice of ¼ lemon
¼ teaspoon English mustard
drizzle of honey
pinch of salt

## Method

Whisk the dressing ingredients together thoroughly in a small bowl.

Combine the salad ingredients in a large serving bowl. If adding fruit, choose only one variety – using all the fruits will make the salad too sweet.

Pour the dressing over the salad just before serving and toss to combine.

Eat the salad on the day of making to ensure the salad leaves stay fresh.

# Vegetable Curries

*Shaak Kari*

It goes without saying that curries are quintessential Indian food. It should come as no surprise then, that curry was an absolute staple of Mum's kitchen. Before putting this chapter together, even I didn't quite appreciate how many ways there are to make a curry.

The tomato 'base' of a curry is often quite similar, so it's the main ingredient that changes the taste and texture. I encourage you to use this base to experiment and create new curries with your favourite vegetables. Some of the vegetables in this section may be difficult to source from your local supermarket, but they can likely be found in an Indian grocery store. I would suggest also sourcing your spices from there, especially ground red chilli, as they are often richer and more pungent. Not all curries are wet either; there's a nice selection of dry curries that skip the tomato 'base' and are cooked in very little liquid, allowing the spices to coat the ingredients directly. They all work really well in a cheese toastie if you have leftovers.

These are simple, weekday recipes that are super easy to bulk up if you're wanting to batch-cook or are having people over to eat. At home, these dishes would be on rotation over 2–3 weeks, as Mum was always changing up her menu and incorporating new ingredients with on-the-spot experimentation. That said, we always stuck to the general unwritten rule of Indian food Monday to Wednesday and Western food for the rest of the week.

SHIV
MCASOL

FRUIT & VEG
AGRUPALMERÍA
Discovered

# Monday Kidney Bean nu Shaak

(Kidney Bean Curry)

Serves 4

Anytime I visit home and Mum asks me what I want to eat, this is always my first choice! It's called Monday kidney bean nu shaak simply because we always ate this on a Monday growing up. If you want to spruce this up some more, add half a tin of sweetcorn – I love the colour, sweetness and added texture it brings to the dish.

## Ingredients

1 white onion, diced
1½ tomatoes, diced
3–4 garlic cloves, minced
2–3 cm (¾–1¼ in) piece of ginger, grated
1 green chilli, finely chopped, to taste
1 tablespoon tomato paste (concentrated puree)
120 g (4½ oz) tinned or frozen sweetcorn (optional)
400 g (14 oz) tinned kidney beans with liquid
½ teaspoon garam masala
10–15 g (¼–½ oz) coriander (cilantro), leaves and stems finely chopped
Everyday Rotli (page 195), to serve

**Vaghaar**

2 tablespoons olive oil
1 teaspoon black mustard seeds
½ teaspoon carom (ajwain) seeds

**Spice Blend**

1 heaped teaspoon ground coriander
1 heaped teaspoon ground cumin
½ teaspoon ground turmeric
½ teaspoon ground red chilli
1–1½ teaspoons salt, to taste

## Method

For the vaghaar, heat the olive oil in a large saucepan over medium heat. Add the mustard seeds and carom seeds and fry, giving the pan a swirl now and then, for 1–2 minutes, or until the mustard seeds start to pop and sizzle.

Stir in the onion, cover with a lid and reduce the heat to low. Simmer for 8–10 minutes, until the onion has softened and browned. Add the tomato, garlic, ginger and chilli and simmer for 2–3 minutes more, then stir in the spice blend, tomato paste and 60–80 ml (¼–⅓ cup) of water. Cover again and simmer for 15 minutes, or until the tomato has softened.

Add the sweetcorn, if using, kidney beans and liquid from the tin. Stir to combine, then increase the heat slightly. Simmer for 8–10 minutes, until the beans have warmed through and softened slightly. Stir in the garam masala and remove from the heat. Add the coriander and stir to combine. Serve with rotli.

## Texts From Home
## Monday Kidney Bean nu Shaak

Heat oil,
fry onions until brown,
add tomatoes,
cook until soft,
add fresh green chilli,
ground red chilli,
dry coriander,
turmeric,
salt
and everything else.

*Mum*

# Heart-Warming Daal

Serves 4–6

My love for this classic Indian dish has only grown since childhood. It's simple, versatile and easy to batch-cook so you can eat it all week long (or freeze it for another time). Don't be afraid to experiment with other vegetables or different types of lentils. This warming staple is perfect for winter, or any occasion when a bit of comfort food is much needed.

## Ingredients

1 white onion, diced

1½ tomatoes, diced

4 garlic cloves, minced

2–3 cm (¾–1¼ in) piece of ginger, grated

1½ green chillies, finely chopped, to taste

300 g (10½ oz) red split lentils (see Notes)

200 ml (7 fl oz) tinned coconut milk (optional)

150 g (3 cups) spinach, roughly chopped (optional)

½ teaspoon garam masala

10–15 g (¼–½ oz) coriander (cilantro), leaves and stems finely chopped

Everyday Rotli (page 195), to serve

aubergine (eggplant) pickle or lime pickle, to serve

**Vaghaar**

2 tablespoons olive oil

1 teaspoon black mustard seeds

1 teaspoon cumin seeds

**Spice Blend**

1 heaped teaspoon ground coriander

1 heaped teaspoon ground cumin

½ teaspoon ground turmeric

1 teaspoon ground red chilli

1–2 teaspoons salt, to taste

## Method

For the vaghaar, heat the olive oil in a large saucepan over medium heat. Add the mustard seeds and cumin seeds and fry, giving the pan a swirl now and then, for 1–2 minutes, until the mustard seeds start to pop and sizzle.

Stir in the onion, cover with a lid and reduce the heat to low. Simmer for 8–10 minutes, until the onion has softened and browned.

Stir in the tomato, garlic, ginger and chilli, cover again and simmer for 8–10 minutes, until the tomato has softened.

Add the spice blend and lentils and stir until the lentils are well coated. Add the coconut milk, if using, for a creamier taste, then top up with enough water to cover the ingredients – the onion will start to float. Cover the pan again and simmer, stirring occasionally and adding more water if the mixture begins to look dry, for 20–30 minutes, or until the lentils are cooked. Add the spinach, if using, and stir until it starts to wilt.

Remove the pan from the heat. If you like, you can use a hand-held blender to create a smoother daal. Stir in the garam masala and coriander.

Serve with rotli and a spoonful of aubergine pickle or lime pickle.

**Notes**

You can replace the red split lentils with chana daal (yellow gram lentils) or yellow split peas. The cooking time will be the same.

My favourite twist on this recipe is adding roasted aubergine (eggplant) or carrot as a topping. Cut the carrot or aubergine into 3.5 cm (1½ in) cubes. Place on a baking tray with a drizzle of olive oil and a sprinkle of salt, pepper and cumin seeds. Roast in a preheated oven at 180°C (350°F) for 20–25 minutes. Scatter over the daal to serve.

You can store leftover daal in an airtight container in the fridge for up to 5 days or in the freezer for up to 6 months.

# Muug

(Green Lentil Curry)

Serves 4–6

This daal is made with green lentils, which are not only packed with iron and antioxidants, but also bring a fresher, earthier flavour to the dish. It's cosy and wholesome just as it is, but you can add a drizzle of double cream if you want it to be a touch more indulgent.

## Ingredients

300 g (10½ oz) green/brown lentils
1 white onion, diced
1½ tomatoes, diced
4 garlic cloves, minced
2–3 cm (¾–1¼ in) piece of ginger, grated
1 green chilli, finely chopped, to taste
½ teaspoon garam masala
10–15 g (¼–½ oz) coriander (cilantro), leaves and stems finely chopped

**Vaghaar**

2 tablespoons olive oil
1 teaspoon black mustard seeds

**Spice Blend**

1 heaped teaspoon ground coriander
1 heaped teaspoon ground cumin
½ teaspoon ground turmeric
1 teaspoon ground red chilli
1–2 teaspoons salt, to taste

**To Serve**

double (heavy) cream or vegan cream (optional)
Everyday Rotli (page 195)
aubergine (eggplant) pickle or lime pickle

## Method

Place the lentils in a large saucepan and add enough cold water to cover them by 4–5 cm (1½–2 in). Soak for at least 2 hours.

After soaking, bring the water to the boil and boil the lentils for 12–15 minutes, until cooked with a slightly mushy consistency. Be sure to use the same water you soaked the lentils in and don't drain the water after cooking. Set aside the pan.

Make the vaghaar by heating the olive oil in a large saucepan over medium heat. Add the mustard seeds and fry, giving the pan a swirl now and then, for 1–2 minutes, until they start to pop and sizzle.

Stir in the onion, reduce the heat to low and cover with a lid. Simmer for 8–10 minutes, until the onion has softened and browned. Stir in the tomato, garlic, ginger and chilli and simmer for 2–3 minutes more. Stir in the spice blend and cover again. Simmer for 15 minutes, or until the tomato has softened.

Stir in the cooked lentils, cover and cook for 6–8 minutes. Stir in the garam masala and remove from the heat.

Add the coriander and stir to combine.

Drizzle cream on top, if you like. Serve with rotli and aubergine pickle or lime pickle.

# Creamy Chana nu Shaak

(Chickpea Curry)

Serves 4

I love how versatile chickpeas are – I don't think I could ever get tired of them. They're a great, nutritious source of protein, so it's no surprise chana is one of the most popular vegetarian Indian curries. You can make this one creamier by adding coconut milk and, as always, feel free to experiment and add any other veg you think might complement the dish, such as aubergine (eggplant) or potato.

## Ingredients

1 white onion, diced

1½ tomatoes, diced

3–4 garlic cloves, minced

2–3 cm (¾–1¼ in) piece of ginger, grated

1 green chilli, finely chopped, to taste

1 tablespoon tomato paste (concentrated puree)

400 g (14 oz) tinned chickpeas (garbanzo beans) with liquid (you can also use black chickpeas)

200 ml (7 fl oz) coconut milk or double (heavy) cream (optional)

150 g (3 cups) spinach, roughly chopped

½ teaspoon garam masala

10–15 g (¼–½ oz) coriander (cilantro), leaves and stems finely chopped

Everyday Rotli (page 195) or steamed basmati rice, to serve

**Vaghaar**

2 tablespoons olive oil

1 teaspoon black mustard seeds

**Spice Blend**

1 heaped teaspoon ground coriander

1 heaped teaspoon ground cumin

½ teaspoon ground turmeric

½ teaspoon ground red chilli

1–1½ teaspoons salt, to taste

## Method

For the vaghaar, heat the olive oil in a large saucepan over medium heat. Add the mustard seeds and fry, giving the pan a swirl now and then, for 1–2 minutes, until they start to pop and sizzle.

Stir in the onion, cover with a lid and simmer over low heat for 8–10 minutes, until the onion has softened and browned. Stir in the tomato, garlic, ginger, chilli, tomato paste and spice blend, then cover and simmer for 12–15 minutes more, until the tomato has softened.

Stir in the chickpeas and chickpea liquid, along with the coconut milk, if using. If you're not adding coconut milk, pour 60–80 ml (¼–⅓ cup) of water into the pan. Add the spinach and stir until it starts to wilt, then stir in the garam masala and remove from the heat. Add the coriander and stir to combine.

Serve with rotli or steamed basmati rice.

How do you want to make the paneer?
Lots of different ways.
x

Block of paneer,
handful of peas,
basic sauce,
can add a little cream.

*Mum*

# Matar Paneer

Serves 4

Paneer is one of those wonderfully versatile ingredients in vegetarian Indian cooking and its mild flavour makes it perfect for soaking up whatever spices you throw at it. This classic dish is another easy, hearty curry that makes a great weekday meal.

## Ingredients

1 tablespoon olive oil

225 g (8 oz) paneer, cut into 2–3 cm (¾–1¼ in) cubes

1 white onion, diced

1 tomato, diced

3–4 garlic cloves, minced

2–3 cm (¾–1¼ in) piece of ginger, grated

1½ green chillies, finely chopped, to taste

1 tablespoon tomato paste (concentrated puree)

150 g (1 cup) frozen peas

100–120 ml (3½–4 fl oz) double (heavy) cream

1 teaspoon honey

½ teaspoon garam masala

10–15 g (¼–½ oz) coriander (cilantro), leaves and stems finely chopped

Everyday Rotli (page 195) and/or Vaghaar Rice (page 210), to serve

**Vaghaar**

2 tablespoons olive oil

1 teaspoon black mustard seeds

1 teaspoon cumin seeds

**Spice Blend**

1 heaped teaspoon ground coriander

1 heaped teaspoon ground cumin

½ teaspoon ground turmeric

½ teaspoon ground red chilli

1–1½ teaspoons salt, to taste

## Method

Heat the olive oil in a large saucepan over medium heat. Add the paneer and fry on each side for 3–4 minutes, until golden brown and crispy. While the paneer is frying, prepare a plate lined with paper towel to absorb any excess oil. Remove the paneer with tongs and transfer to the paper towel.

For the vaghaar, heat the olive oil in a large saucepan over medium heat. Add the mustard seeds and cumin seeds and fry, giving the pan a swirl now and then, for 1–2 minutes, until the mustard seeds start to pop and sizzle.

Stir in the onion, reduce the heat to low and cover with a lid. Simmer for 8–10 minutes, until the onion has softened and browned. Stir in the tomato, garlic, ginger, chilli, tomato paste and spice blend, then cover and simmer for 12–15 minutes, until the tomato has softened.

Stir in the paneer, peas, cream, honey and 60–80 ml (¼–⅓ cup) of water and cook for a further 5 minutes, or until the peas have defrosted. Add more water if the curry sauce looks too dry. Stir in the garam masala and remove from the heat. Add the coriander and stir to combine.

Serve with rotli and/or vaghaar rice.

# Inda nu Shaak

(Egg Curry)

Serves 4

Egg curry has really grown on me over the years, as I only used to like scrambled eggs or the whites of an egg. There are a few variations in this book that may take you by surprise, with a recipe to accommodate your favourite type of egg – boiled, poached or scrambled. This protein-packed dish, bulked up with potato and spinach, is best served with *Everyday Rotli* (page 195) and/or steamed basmati rice.

## Ingredients

6 eggs

300 g (10½ oz) all-purpose potatoes, peeled and cut into 3.5–4 cm (1½ in) cubes

2 tablespoons olive oil

1 white onion, diced

2 tomatoes, diced

2–3 garlic cloves, minced

2–3 cm (¾–1¼ in) piece of ginger, grated

2 green chillies, finely chopped, to taste

200 g (4 cups) spinach, roughly chopped

10–15 g (¼–½ oz) coriander (cilantro), leaves and stems finely chopped

Everyday Rotli (page 195) and/or steamed basmati rice, to serve

**Spice Blend**

1 heaped teaspoon ground coriander

1 heaped teaspoon ground cumin

1 teaspoon ground turmeric

½ teaspoon garam masala

1 teaspoon ground red chilli

1–1½ teaspoons salt, to taste

## Method

Bring a large saucepan of water to the boil. Once boiling, add the eggs and potato to the pan and boil for 8–10 minutes. Drain and set aside to cool.

Heat the olive oil in a large saucepan over medium heat. Stir in the onion, reduce the heat to low and cover with a lid. Simmer for 8–10 minutes, until the onion has softened and browned. Stir in the tomato, garlic, ginger, chilli and spice blend. Cover, increase the heat to medium-low and simmer for 10–12 minutes, until the tomato has softened.

Meanwhile, peel the eggs and cut them into quarters.

Add the eggs and potato to the sauce, along with the spinach and 60–80 ml (¼–⅓ cup) of water. Stir to combine and cook for 5 minutes more.

Remove from the heat, add the coriander and stir to combine.

Serve with rotli and/or basmati rice.

# Ringan nu Shaak (Aubergine Curry)

Serves 6

Once you've got the knack for cooking it, aubergine really is a top-tier vegetable, and this curry proves just that. Try smoking or roasting the aubergine before adding it into the curry sauce for a different but equally delicious flavour. The addition of peas and potato gives a nice blend of textures and adds a pop of colour.

## Ingredients

2 tomatoes, diced

1 tablespoon tomato paste (concentrated puree)

3–4 garlic cloves, minced

2–3 cm (¾–1¼ in) piece of ginger, grated

1 green chilli, finely chopped, to taste

2 large aubergines (eggplants), cut into 2.5–3 cm (1–1¼ in) cubes (see Note)

1 large all-purpose potato, peeled and cut into 2.5–3 cm (1–1¼ in) cubes

300 g (2 cups) frozen peas

½ teaspoon garam masala

10–15 g (¼–½ oz) coriander (cilantro), leaves and stems finely chopped

Everyday Rotli (page 195), to serve

Sweet & Tangy Apple Chutney (page 238), to serve

**Vaghaar**

2 tablespoons olive oil

1 teaspoon black mustard seeds

1 teaspoon cumin seeds

½ teaspoon asafoetida (optional)

**Spice Blend**

1 heaped teaspoon ground coriander

1 heaped teaspoon ground cumin

½ teaspoon ground turmeric

1 teaspoon ground red chilli

1–2 teaspoons salt, to taste

## Method

For the vaghaar, heat the olive oil in a large saucepan over medium heat. Add the mustard seeds, cumin seeds and asafoetida, if using, and fry, giving the pan a swirl now and then, for 1–2 minutes, until the mustard seeds start to pop and sizzle.

Stir in the tomato, tomato paste, garlic, ginger, chilli and spice blend. Cover, increase the heat to medium-low and simmer for 10–12 minutes, until the tomato has softened.

Next stir in the aubergine, potato, peas and 200 ml (7 fl oz) of water. Cover with a lid and simmer for 12–15 minutes or until the aubergine and potato are cooked.

Stir in the garam masala and remove from the heat.

Add the coriander and stir to combine.

Serve with rotli and apple chutney.

**Note**

If you'd like to smoke the aubergines, pierce them several times and place directly on separate gas rings over a high flame. Cook for 8 minutes each side, turning with tongs, then set aside to cool. Once cool, split lengthways, scoop out the flesh and discard as much burnt skin as possible. Alternatively, roast at 220–240°C (430–465°F) for 30–40 minutes, though the flavour will be less smoky.

# Batata nu Shaak

(Potato Curry)

Serves 4

This nourishing dish of Gujarati comfort food doesn't hold back on the carb content, as it is usually served with *Everyday Rotli* or *Poori*. If you want a bit more variation in flavour and texture, I recommend using a mix of all-purpose potatoes and sweet potatoes and adding the peas and spinach.

## Ingredients

1 white onion, diced
4–5 garlic cloves, minced
2–3 cm (¾–1¼ in) piece of ginger, grated
1 green chilli, finely chopped, to taste
3–4 makrut lime leaves
500 g (1 lb 2 oz) all-purpose potatoes, peeled and cut into 3.5–4 cm (1½ in) cubes
1½ tomatoes, diced
300 g (2 cups) frozen peas (optional)
300 g (6 cups) spinach, roughly chopped (optional)
10–15 g (¼–½ oz) coriander (cilantro), leaves and stems finely chopped
Everyday Rotli (page 195) or Poori (page 196), to serve

**Vaghaar**

2 tablespoons olive oil
1 teaspoon black mustard seeds
1 teaspoon cumin seeds

**Spice Blend**

1 heaped teaspoon ground coriander
1 heaped teaspoon ground cumin
1 teaspoon ground turmeric
1 teaspoon garam masala
1 teaspoon ground red chilli
1–2 teaspoons salt, to taste

## Method

For the vaghaar, heat the olive oil in a large saucepan over medium heat. Add the mustard seeds and cumin seeds and fry, giving the pan a swirl now and then, for 1–2 minutes, until the mustard seeds start to pop and sizzle.

Stir in the onion, reduce the heat to low and cover with a lid. Simmer for 8–10 minutes, until the onion has softened and browned. Stir in the garlic, ginger, chilli, makrut lime leaves, potato and spice blend, making sure the potato is well coated in the spices. Cook for 3–4 minutes.

Add the tomato, along with the peas and spinach, if using, and 200 ml (7 fl oz) of water. Stir, cover again and simmer for 20 minutes, or until the tomato and potato have softened.

Remove from the heat, add the coriander and stir to combine.

Serve alongside plenty of rotli or poori.

# Ringan Palita nu Shaak

(Aubergine & Potato Curry)

Serves 4

Potato and aubergine has to be my all-time favourite veg pairing. This traditional Gujarati dry curry is quick, homely and one of my go-to weekday dinners. It can be enjoyed on its own or with your classic rotli.

## Ingredients

2 tablespoons olive oil

1 tablespoon gram (besan) flour

3–4 garlic cloves, minced

2–3 cm (¾–1¼ in) piece of ginger, grated

1 green chilli, finely chopped

2 small aubergines (eggplants), cut into 5 mm–1 cm (¼–½ in) thick slices

1 large all-purpose potato, peeled and cut into 5 mm–1 cm (¼–½ in) thick slices

**Vaghaar**

2 tablespoons olive oil

1 teaspoon black mustard seeds

1 teaspoon cumin seeds

**Spice Blend**

1 teaspoon ground coriander

1 teaspoon ground cumin

¼ teaspoon ground turmeric

½ teaspoon garam masala

½ teaspoon ground red chilli

1–2 teaspoons salt, to taste

**To Serve**

finely chopped coriander (cilantro), leaves and stems

Everyday Rotli (page 195) (optional)

Fresh Green Chutney (page 234) or Mint Yoghurt (page 231) (optional)

## Method

Whisk the olive oil, gram flour, garlic, ginger, chilli, spice blend and 60 ml (¼ cup) of water together in a mixing bowl to form a marinade.

Use a basting brush to evenly coat the aubergine and potato slices with the marinade. Set aside.

For the vaghaar, heat the olive oil in a large frying pan over medium heat. Add the mustard seeds and cumin seeds and fry, giving the pan a swirl now and then, for 2 minutes, or until the mustard seeds start to pop and sizzle.

Add the marinated aubergine and potato to the pan with 60–80 ml (¼–⅓ cup) of water – this will ensure there is enough moisture, as the vaghaar will be quickly absorbed by the vegetables. Cover the pan with a lid, reduce the heat to medium–low and cook for 10–12 minutes, before turning the slices. Cook without the lid for 10–12 minutes more. The slices will be soft inside and golden brown on the outside when ready.

Remove from the heat and scatter the coriander on top. Serve the curry with rotli or on its own dipped into green chutney or mint yoghurt.

Royal Vine

# Vadhu nu Shaak

(Sprouted Mung Bean Curry)

Serves 4

This curry's cooking process is a little longer than average as you have to wait for the beans to sprout, but it's a tasty, healthy option that can be enjoyed hot or cold. My maa made this more frequently than my mum, and would often send us on our way with it in a pack-up.

## Ingredients

1 white onion, diced

2–3 garlic cloves, minced

2–3 cm (¾–1¼ in) piece of ginger, grated

2 green chillies, finely chopped, to taste

10–15 g (¼–½ oz) coriander (cilantro), leaves and stems finely chopped

Everyday Rotli (page 195), to serve

**Bean & Lentil Mix** (see Note opposite)

50 g (1¾ oz) mung beans

50 g (1¾ oz) brown/green lentils

30 g (1 oz) vaal (field beans/dried broad/fava beans)

30 g (1 oz) dried white chickpeas (garbanzo beans)

30 g (1 oz) dried black chickpeas

25 g (1 oz) moth beans

25 g (1 oz) black-eye beans

**Vaghaar**

2 tablespoons olive oil

1 teaspoon black mustard seeds

**Spice Blend**

1 heaped teaspoon ground coriander

1 heaped teaspoon ground cumin

½ teaspoon ground turmeric

½ teaspoon garam masala

1 teaspoon ground red chilli

1 teaspoon salt, to taste

## Method

### Day 1

Wash and soak the bean and lentil mix in warm water in a large bowl. Set aside.

### Day 2

The next day, drain the water off and tie the mixture in a tea towel or muslin cloth. Leave the mixture in a warm, dry place for another 1–2 days, until the beans and lentils start to sprout. Check them after 12 hours. The sprouting time will vary depending on room temperature and can therefore take longer in colder climates or in the winter months. My maa's trick is to place them near a heater (boiler).

### Day 3

Once most of the beans and lentils have sprouted, wash them in hot water before cooking.

For the vaghaar, heat the olive oil in a large saucepan over medium heat. Add the mustard seeds and fry, giving the pan a swirl now and then, for 1–2 minutes, until the mustard seeds start to pop and sizzle.

Stir in the onion, reduce the heat to low and cover with a lid. Simmer for 8–10 minutes, until the onion has softened and browned. Stir in the beans and lentils, along with the garlic, ginger and chilli and cook for 2–3 minutes. Add the spice blend and stir well until the mixture is coated. Add enough water to cover the beans and lentils by 1 cm (½ in), increase the heat to medium-low and cover again. Simmer for 25–30 minutes, until the beans and lentils are soft. Add more water if the beans start to stick to the pan.

Remove from the heat, add the coriander and stir to combine.

Serve hot or cold with rotli.

### Note

Some of the beans can be harder to find, so you don't need to use every type – just keep the overall quantity the same. Many Indian grocers sell a 'vadhu mix', which I highly recommend looking for. The most important bean is mung, so be sure to include that in your mix.

RAVAYA
Nature enjoy!
STER
GUVAR 6.99/Kg

# Guvar nu Shaak

(Cluster Bean Curry)

Serves 4

This recipe is known as 'stick nu shaak', or 'stick curry', in our household. Cluster beans are a staple in Gujarati cuisine. They are full of fibre, vitamin C and antioxidants. Be sure not to confuse them with green beans; although they are related, cluster beans are smaller, flatter and have a slightly bitter taste.

## Ingredients

350 g (12½ oz) fresh or frozen cluster beans (guvar)

1 white onion, diced

60 g (2 oz) frozen peas

2–3 garlic cloves, minced

2–3 cm (¾–1¼ in) piece of ginger, grated

1 green chilli, finely chopped, to taste

10–15 g (¼–½ oz) coriander (cilantro), leaves and stems finely chopped

Everyday Rotli (page 195), to serve

Muug (page 135), to serve (optional)

**Vaghaar**

2 tablespoons olive oil

½ teaspoon carom (ajwain) seeds

**Spice Blend**

1 heaped teaspoon ground coriander

1 heaped teaspoon ground cumin

½ teaspoon ground turmeric

½ teaspoon ground red chilli

1–1½ teaspoons salt, to taste

## Method

If using fresh cluster beans, first wash, dry and cut the ends off the beans. Snap the bean stems in half and set aside.

For the vaghaar, heat the olive oil in a large saucepan over medium heat. Add the carom seeds and fry, giving the pan a swirl now and then, for 1–2 minutes, until their aroma is released. As soon as you start to smell the spice, the vaghaar is ready – you don't want to burn the spice.

Stir in the onion, reduce the heat to low and cover with a lid. Simmer for 8–10 minutes, until the onion has softened and browned. Stir in the cluster beans, frozen peas, garlic, ginger, chilli and spice blend, cover with a lid and cook for 10–15 minutes, stirring occasionally, until the cluster beans start to soften.

Remove the pan from the heat, add the coriander and stir to combine.

Serve with rotli. This dish pairs well with muug daal.

# Cauliflower & Mix Veg Curry

Serves 4

This is not just a great dinner option, it's also my favourite cheese toastie filling! I would highly recommend trying this with your leftovers. The mix of vegetables brings a lovely burst of colour, which is something you don't often see in tomato-based curries. I love bulking this up with all kinds of veg – green beans and courgettes (zucchini) are great – though it works beautifully as a solo cauliflower dish too.

## Ingredients

1 large cauliflower, florets cut off

1 carrot, diced

1 small all-purpose potato, peeled and diced

60 g (2 oz) frozen peas

60 g (2 oz) frozen sweetcorn

3–4 garlic cloves, minced

2–3 cm (¾–1¼ in) piece of ginger, grated

1 green chilli, finely chopped

1 tomato, diced

10–15 g (¼–½ oz) coriander (cilantro), leaves and stems finely chopped

Sweet & Tangy Apple Chutney (page 238), to serve

Everyday Rotli (page 195) or Poori (page 196), to serve

**Vaghaar**

2 tablespoons olive oil

1 teaspoon black mustard seeds

1 teaspoon cumin seeds

**Spice Blend**

1 heaped teaspoon ground coriander

1 heaped teaspoon ground cumin

½ teaspoon ground turmeric

1 teaspoon ground red chilli

1–2 teaspoons salt, to taste

## Method

For the vaghaar, heat the olive oil in a large saucepan over medium heat. Add the mustard seeds and cumin seeds and fry, giving the pan a swirl now and then, for 1–2 minutes, until the mustard seeds start to pop and sizzle.

Add the cauliflower, carrot, potato, peas, sweetcorn, garlic, ginger and chilli and stir well. Cook for 4–5 minutes, then stir in the spice blend. Cook for 5 minutes more, then stir in the tomato and 60–80 ml (¼–⅓ cup) of water, cover with a lid and reduce the heat to medium-low. Cook for 15 minutes, or until the potato is soft.

Remove the pan from the heat, add the coriander and stir to combine.

Serve with apple chutney and some rotli or poori alongside.

Texts From Home
Bhaji nu Shaak

Oil,
dry methi,
add chopped bhaji,
onions,
add all-spices
and cook.
x

*Mum*

# Bhaji nu Shaak

(Spinach Curry)

Serves 4 *(As a side dish)*

Spinach itself can be mixed into most of the curries in this book, but this recipe spotlights the beloved leafy green as the main attraction. Don't be shy with the oil when making this one, as you don't want the spinach to dry up. This makes a great side dish to bring to a dinner party.

## Ingredients

1 white onion, diced
500 g (1 lb 2 oz) spinach, roughly chopped
4 garlic cloves, minced
2–3 cm (¾–1¼ in) piece of ginger, grated
1 green chilli, finely chopped, to taste

**Vaghaar**
2–3 tablespoons olive oil
½ teaspoon fenugreek seeds

**Spice Blend**
1 heaped teaspoon ground coriander
1 heaped teaspoon ground cumin
½ teaspoon ground turmeric
½ teaspoon ground red chilli
1 teaspoon salt, to taste

## Method

For the vaghaar, heat the olive oil in a saucepan over medium heat. Add the fenugreek seeds and fry, giving the pan a swirl now and then, for 2 minutes, or until they start to brown and become fragrant.

Stir in the onion, reduce the heat to low and cover with a lid. Simmer for 8–10 minutes, until the onion has softened and browned. Stir in the spinach, garlic, ginger, chilli and spice blend and increase the heat to medium. Simmer, uncovered, for 10 minutes, or until the spinach has wilted. You may need to add a splash of water if the spinach starts to dry out.

Serve as a side dish to accompany any curry in this book.

**Note**

Try these variations to mix things up:

Add 1 potato, peeled and cut into 2–3 cm (¾–1¼ in) cubes, and a handful of frozen peas to the pan when you add the spinach. Cook, covered, for 12–15 minutes, or until the potato is cooked.

Cut 200 g (7 oz) of paneer into 2–3 cm (¾–1¼ in) cubes. Heat 1 tablespoon of olive oil in a frying pan over medium heat. Add the paneer cubes and fry on each side for 3–4 minutes, until golden brown and crispy. Add the paneer to the curry at the end of cooking.

# Bhinda nu Shaak

(Okra Curry)

Serves 4

Growing up, I only knew the Gujarati name for most foods – so it wasn't until my teens that I realised bhinda was called 'lady's fingers' or 'okra' in English. Regardless of the name, it's such an underrated vegetable. Just don't forget to add a squeeze of lemon to prevent it from becoming too slimy.

## Ingredients

400 g (14 oz) okra (bhinda)

1 white onion, diced

juice of ½ lemon, plus ½ lemon more, to serve

2–3 garlic cloves, minced

2–3 cm (¾–1¼ in) piece of ginger, grated

1 green chilli, finely chopped, to taste

1 all-purpose potato, peeled and cut into 3–4 cm 1¼–1½ in) cubes (optional)

10–15 g (¼–½ oz) coriander (cilantro), leaves and stems finely chopped

**Vaghaar**

2 tablespoons olive oil

½ teaspoon fenugreek seeds

**Spice Blend**

1 heaped teaspoon ground coriander

1 heaped teaspoon ground cumin

¼ teaspoon ground turmeric

½ teaspoon ground red chilli

1 teaspoon salt, to taste

**To Serve**

Everyday Rotli (page 195) or Poori (page 196)

aubergine (eggplant) pickle or lime pickle

Heart-Warming Daal (page 130; optional)

## Method

Wash and thoroughly dry the okra with a tea towel before cutting them diagonally into thin rounds.

For the vaghaar, heat the olive oil in a large saucepan over medium heat. Add the fenugreek seeds and fry, giving the pan a swirl now and then, for 2 minutes, or until they start to brown and become fragrant.

Stir in the onion, lemon juice, garlic, ginger, chilli and spice blend and cook for 4–5 minutes. If using the potato, add it now, cover the pan and cook for an extra 6–8 minutes, or until the potato is soft.

Stir in the okra and cook, stirring occasionally, for 10–15 minutes, until it starts to soften.

Remove the pan from the heat, add the coriander and stir to combine.

Serve with rotli or poori and aubergine pickle or lime pickle. This curry also pairs well with heart-warming daal.

# Meat & Seafood Curries

*Gosht & Machali Kari*

Chicken tikka masala is widely considered to be Britain's national dish. It's a great example of the impact Asian cuisine has had on native taste buds and vice versa – the dish itself originated in the UK, adapted from its Indian origins to better suit British palates. As Gujaratis are traditionally vegetarian, and my food preferences also tend in that direction, the vegetable chapter is the larger of the two curry sections in this book. But there is still a solid selection of meat-based curries to get stuck into here, thanks to the meat-loving members of my family.

Dad has always been a particularly big fan of meat-based dishes. He often reminisces about going out for weekly drinks with his friends and returning to one of their houses to be met with a delicious lamb or chicken dish, accompanied with a loaf of bread that was left out for them. While it might sound like a dated tradition now, in Gujarati culture it's unheard of for a wife to go to bed without preparing dinner for her husband. Thankfully, my dad and his friends would return the favour by washing up before they left.

There's only one way to cook each type of meat here, unlike a typical Indian takeaway where you might be able to pick between a bhuna, korma or balti sauce, for example. Although some of these might be considered less indulgent than what you would get dining out, they are generally healthier and meet the overall theme of wholesome home cooking that runs throughout this book.

# Heart-Warming Chicken Curry

Serves 6

This comforting curry was a bi-weekly staple in our household – I specifically remember eating this on Wednesdays. It is one of the few dishes enjoyed equally by all my family members, despite mine and my sister's differing tastes. I love adding potatoes, which provide substance and a nice textural contrast.

## Ingredients

700–800 g (1 lb 9 oz–1 lb 12 oz) bone-in, skinless chicken thighs (see Notes)

5–6 curry leaves

1 white onion, diced

1½ tomatoes, diced

6 garlic cloves, minced

2–3 cm (¾–1¼ in) piece of ginger, grated

2 green chillies, finely chopped, to taste

1 tablespoon tomato paste (concentrated puree)

½ teaspoon garam masala

10–15 g (¼–½ oz) coriander (cilantro), leaves and stems finely chopped

lemon wedges, to serve

Yoghurt Naan Bread (page 198) or steamed basmati rice smothered in butter, to serve

**Vaghaar**

3 tablespoons olive oil

3–4 whole cloves

½ cinnamon stick

**Spice Blend**

1 heaped teaspoon ground coriander

1 heaped teaspoon ground cumin

1 teaspoon ground turmeric

½ teaspoon ground red chilli

2 teaspoons salt, to taste

## Method

Cut the chicken thighs into 4–5 cm (1½–2 in) pieces with the bone left in and trim the fat off. Wash the chicken and pat it dry with paper towel.

For the vaghaar, heat the olive oil in a large saucepan over medium heat. Add the cloves and cinnamon stick and fry, giving the pan a swirl now and then, for 2 minutes, or until their aromas are released. As soon as you start to smell the spices the vaghaar is ready – you don't want to burn the spices.

Stir in the curry leaves and onion, reduce the heat to low and cover with a lid. Simmer for 10 minutes, or until the onion has softened and browned. Stir in the tomato, garlic, ginger, chilli and spice blend and cover again. Simmer for 7 minutes, stirring occasionally, then stir in the tomato paste. Continue to simmer for 8 minutes with the lid on, stirring occasionally, until the tomato has softened.

Add the chicken, give everything a stir and cook for another 15 minutes with the lid on. Add 120–150 ml (4–5 fl oz) of water (depending on how saucy you like your curry), increase the heat to medium-low, cover and cook for another 12–15 minutes.

Remove the cloves and cinnamon stick. Stir in the garam masala and remove the pan from the heat. Add the coriander and stir to combine.

Serve with lemon wedges and naan or rice.

**Notes**

You can also use a mix of chicken breasts, thighs and wings – ask your butcher to prepare the chicken for you with the bones in.

To change things up you can add 1 tablespoon of store-bought tandoori paste when you add the tomato paste for a slightly different taste.

If you like, add 1 large potato, peeled and cut into 3.5–4 cm (1½ in) chunks, when you add the chicken.

# Dada's Lamb Curry

Serves 6

My late dada loved making this curry for large family get-togethers, cooking it in a triple-sized metal pot over his makeshift garage stove (something that definitely wouldn't meet today's safety standards). It was always too oily and too spicy, but everyone went back for more, especially to fight over the prized bone marrow pieces. Dada always preferred using mutton, which I'd recommend too, and liked to serve the curry with *Poora*.

## Ingredients

900 g (2 lb) lamb leg or shoulder, bone-in (see Notes)

1 white onion, diced

1½ tomatoes, roughly chopped

½ aubergine (eggplant), roughly chopped

6 garlic cloves, roughly chopped

2–3 cm (¾–1¼ in) piece of ginger, roughly chopped

2 green chillies, roughly chopped, to taste

1 tablespoon tomato paste (concentrated puree)

½ teaspoon garam masala

10–15 g (¼–½ oz) coriander (cilantro), leaves and stems finely chopped

lemon wedges, to serve

Poora (page 203) or steamed basmati rice smothered in butter, to serve

**Vaghaar**

3 tablespoons olive oil

3–4 whole cloves

1 small cinnamon stick

2 whole star anise

1–2 bay leaves

**Spice Blend**

1 heaped teaspoon ground coriander

1 heaped teaspoon ground cumin

1 teaspoon ground turmeric

½ teaspoon ground red chilli

1–2 teaspoons salt, to taste

## Method

Cut the lamb into small pieces with the bone left in and trim the fat off. Wash the lamb and pat it dry with paper towel.

For the vaghaar, heat the olive oil in a large saucepan over medium heat. Add the cloves, cinnamon stick, star anise and bay leaves and fry, giving the pan a swirl now and then, for 2 minutes, or until their aromas are released. As soon as you start to smell the spices the vaghaar is ready – you don't want to burn the spices.

Stir in the onion, reduce the heat to low and cover with a lid. Simmer for 8–10 minutes, until the onion has softened and browned.

Blitz the tomato, aubergine, garlic, ginger and chilli in a food processor to form a puree. Add the puree and spice blend to the onion and stir thoroughly. Cover and simmer for 8 minutes, stirring occasionally, then stir in the tomato paste. Continue to simmer for 8 minutes more with the lid on, stirring occasionally, until the tomato has softened.

Stir the lamb through the sauce, then cook for 45–60 minutes, until the lamb is tender. Add 120–150 ml (4–5 fl oz) of water halfway through cooking to ensure the curry doesn't dry out.

Remove the cloves, cinnamon stick, star anise and bay leaves. Stir in the garam masala and remove from the heat. Add the coriander and stir to combine.

Serve with lemon wedges alongside poora or steamed basmati rice smothered in butter.

**Notes**

You can ask the butcher to prepare the lamb for you.

You can also substitute the lamb for goat or mutton.

Texts From Home
Masala Roast Chicken

Mix spices together
and cover the chicken
and put some inside the carcass as well …
foil and roast.
Use sauce as gravy.
Xx

*Maya Masi*

# Masala Roast Chicken

Serves 4–6

Fancy a Gujarati-style Christmas? This masala roast chicken is a Lad family tradition, usually made by one of my masis (my aunts on my mum's side). My cousins refuse to eat roast chicken any other way! Serve it with the usual Christmas trimmings or use the same marinade on chicken fillets and enjoy it with *Everyday Rotli* or *Yoghurt Naan Bread*.

## Ingredients

1 × 1.2–1.5 kg (2 lb 10 oz–3 lb 5 oz) whole chicken

2 white onions, quartered

5–6 garlic cloves, unpeeled

Everyday Rotli (page 195) or Yoghurt Naan Bread (page 198), to serve (optional)

**Marinade**

2 tablespoons olive oil

3–4 garlic cloves, minced

3–4 cm (1¼–1½ in) piece of ginger, grated

1 green chilli, finely chopped, to taste

1 heaped teaspoon ground coriander

1 heaped teaspoon ground cumin

1 teaspoon ground turmeric

1 teaspoon garam masala

1 teaspoon ground red chilli

1 teaspoon ground black pepper

2 teaspoons salt, to taste

## Method

Preheat the oven to 200°C (400°F).

Combine the marinade ingredients together in a bowl. You may need to add an extra drizzle of oil to loosen up the spices.

Use a basting brush to evenly coat the chicken with the marinade, making sure to get under the skin by carefully holding the skin at the tip of the chicken breasts, pulling up gently (making sure it doesn't tear) and using your other hand to separate the skin from the meat of the breast. Use your fingers to rub a little marinade inside.

Place the chicken in a roasting tin, along with the onion and unpeeled garlic. Cover with foil and cook for 40 minutes.

Remove the foil and roast for 15–20 minutes more, until the chicken is cooked and the skin is crispy. You can check the chicken is cooked by piercing it with a skewer at the thickest part – if the juices run clear it is done.

Remove the roast chicken from the oven and allow it to rest for 5–10 minutes before carving and serving with all the Christmas trimmings! Alternatively, enjoy it anytime of the year with rotli or naan.

# Jinga

(Prawn Curry)

Serves 4

Prawns are my absolute favourite seafood – I could happily eat them every day. To make this recipe creamier, try adding coconut milk or powder (admittedly, this is a South Indian way of cooking, however it's too delicious not to suggest).

## Ingredients

5–6 curry leaves

1 white onion, diced

2 tomatoes, diced

6 garlic cloves, minced

2–3 cm (¾–1¼ in) piece of ginger, grated

2 green chillies, finely chopped, to taste

1 tablespoon tomato paste (concentrated puree)

400–500 g (14–1 lb 2 oz) fresh or frozen king prawns (jumbo shrimp)

½ teaspoon garam masala

½ lemon, plus lemon wedges, to serve

10–15 g (¼–½ oz) coriander (cilantro), leaves and stems finely chopped

Everyday Rotli (page 195) and/or steamed basmati rice smothered in butter

**Vaghaar**

2 tablespoons olive oil

½ teaspoon black mustard seeds

½ cinnamon stick

**Spice Blend**

1 heaped teaspoon ground coriander

1 heaped teaspoon ground cumin

½ teaspoon ground turmeric

½ teaspoon ground red chilli

1–2 teaspoons salt, to taste

## Method

For the vaghaar, heat the olive oil in a large saucepan over medium heat. Add the mustard seeds and cinnamon stick and fry, giving the pan a swirl now and then, for 1–2 minutes, until the mustard seeds start to pop and sizzle.

Stir in the curry leaves and onion, reduce the heat to low and cover with a lid. Simmer for 8–10 minutes, until the onion has softened and browned. Add the tomato, garlic, ginger, chilli and spice blend and stir well. Cover and simmer for 8 minutes, stirring occasionally, then stir in the tomato paste. Continue to simmer, covered, for 8 minutes, or until the tomato has softened.

Remove the lid. Stir in 120–150 ml (4–5 fl oz) of water, add the prawns and cook for 5 minutes if fresh or 10 minutes if frozen – don't overcook the prawns. Remove the cinnamon stick. Stir in the garam masala and remove the pan from the heat. Squeeze the lemon half over the curry and stir through the coriander. Serve with lemon wedges and rotli and/or steamed basmati rice smothered in butter.

**Note**

For a creamier taste, add 2 tablespoons of coconut milk powder when you add the water or replace the water with 120–150 ml (4–5 fl oz) of coconut milk.

# Fish Curry

Serves 4

I personally prefer a fish curry to a meat one. I love how versatile it can be – using different types of fish can completely change the flavour. My mum and I often use haddock or cod, but salmon works just as well. I'd encourage you to use whichever fish you like best. For a creamier taste, add 2 tablespoons of coconut milk powder when you add the water or replace the water with 120–150 ml (4–5 fl oz) of coconut milk.

## Ingredients

1½ tomatoes, diced

6 garlic cloves, minced

2–3 cm (¾–1¼ in) piece of ginger, grated

1½ green chillies, finely chopped, to taste

1 tablespoon tomato paste (concentrated puree)

4 × 125 g (4½ oz) skin-on, firm white fish fillets, cut into 6–8 cm (2½–3¼ in) chunks

½ teaspoon garam masala

½ lemon, plus lemon wedges to serve

10–15 g (¼–½ oz) coriander (cilantro), leaves and stems finely chopped

Everyday Rotli (page 195) or Vaghaar Rice (page 210), to serve

**Vaghaar**

2 tablespoons olive oil

½ teaspoon fenugreek seeds

5–6 curry leaves

**Spice Blend**

1 heaped teaspoon ground coriander

1 heaped teaspoon ground cumin

1 teaspoon ground turmeric

½ teaspoon ground red chilli

1–2 teaspoons salt, to taste

## Method

For the vaghaar, heat the olive oil in a large saucepan over medium heat. Add the fenugreek seeds and curry leaves and fry, giving the pan a swirl now and then, for 2 minutes, or until they start to brown slightly and their aroma is released.

Add the tomato, garlic, ginger, chilli and spice blend to the pan and stir thoroughly. Reduce the heat to medium–low and cover with a lid. Simmer for 8 minutes, stirring occasionally, then stir in the tomato paste. Continue to simmer for 8 minutes more with the lid on, stirring occasionally, until the tomato has softened.

Stir in 120–150 ml (4–5 fl oz) of water, add the fish and cook for 10 minutes more with the lid on.

Stir in the garam masala, then remove the pan from the heat. Squeeze the lemon half over the curry, add the coriander and stir to combine.

Serve with lemon wedges and rotli or vaghaar rice.

# Spicy Lemon Salmon

Serves 4

This is my absolute favourite way to cook salmon – simple, flavourful and endlessly versatile. As with the fish curry opposite, try using this marinade on your favourite type of fish. My dad loves to eat it directly out of the pan so he can soak up the delicious marinade with his rotli or bread.

## Ingredients

4 × 100–150 g (3½–5 oz) skin-on salmon fillets (see Note overleaf)

3–4 spring onions (scallions), chopped

10–15 g (¼–½ oz) coriander (cilantro), leaves and stems finely chopped

juice of ½ lemon, plus lemon wedges to serve

Everyday Rotli (page 195) and/or steamed basmati rice smothered in butter, to serve

Versatile Salad (page 118) or a green leafy salad, to serve (optional)

**Marinade**

1 tablespoon olive oil

4 garlic cloves, minced

2–3 cm (¾–1¼ in) piece of ginger, grated

3–4 green chillies, finely chopped, to taste

10–15 g (¼–½ oz) coriander (cilantro), leaves and stems finely chopped

juice of 1 lemon

1 heaped teaspoon ground coriander

1 heaped teaspoon ground cumin

1 teaspoon ground turmeric

1 teaspoon garam masala

1 teaspoon ground red chilli

1–2 teaspoons salt, to taste

**Vaghaar**

2 tablespoons olive oil

½ teaspoon fenugreek seeds

4–5 curry leaves

Buy fish,
do a marinade with lemon.
Salt,
turmeric,
green chilli,
ground red chilli,
coriander,
garam masala (only a little bit).

*Mum*

## Method

You can chop the salmon into bite-sized chunks or leave the fillets whole – it's up to you.

Combine the marinade ingredients in a large airtight container with a lid. You may need to add an extra drizzle of olive oil to loosen up the spices. Add the salmon and give everything a mix, making sure the fish is evenly coated in the marinade. Seal with the lid and place in the fridge to marinate for at least 3 hours, but leave overnight for the best results.

For the vaghaar, heat the olive oil in a large saucepan over medium heat. Add the fenugreek seeds and fry, giving the pan a swirl now and then, for 2 minutes, or until they brown and become fragrant. Add the curry leaves and cook for 1 minute more.

Add the marinated salmon, reduce the heat to low and cover with a lid. Simmer for 6–8 minutes, then remove the lid and add most of the spring onion.

Use tongs to turn each piece of fish over, then increase the heat to medium and cook for another 6–8 minutes.

Remove from the heat, add the remaining spring onion, the coriander and lemon juice and stir to combine.

Serve with lemon wedges on the side. Enjoy the salmon on its own or with rotli and/or steamed basmati rice. It's also great with a fresh salad.

**Note**

You can swap the salmon out for rainbow (steelhead) trout, barramundi or flathead if you're in Australia or haddock or cod if you're in the Northern Hemisphere.

# Crab Curry

Serves 4–6

We don't make this recipe often – not because it's hard to cook, but because it's wonderfully messy to eat. Adding some crabmeat into the curry as it cooks helps to thicken the sauce and makes it even richer. It can be very helpful to have the correct utensils, particularly a crab cracker and seafood fork, to scoop out the delicious crabmeat. I like to do this step first, clear the shells from my plate and give it a quick reheat in the microwave. It's worth every bit of effort!

## Ingredients

8–10 whole crab claws (about 900 g/2 lbs)
3–4 curry leaves
4–5 cm (1½–2 in) piece of ginger, grated
1 white onion, diced
2 tomatoes, diced
6 garlic cloves, minced
3 green chillies, finely chopped, to taste
1 tablespoon tomato paste (concentrated puree)
½ teaspoon garam masala
½ lemon, plus lemon wedges to serve
10–15 g (¼–½ oz) coriander (cilantro), leaves and stems finely chopped
Yoghurt Naan Bread (page 198) and/or steamed basmati rice smothered in butter

**Vaghaar**

2 tablespoons olive oil
1 large cinnamon stick
3 whole cloves

**Spice Blend**

1 heaped teaspoon ground coriander
1 heaped teaspoon ground cumin
1 teaspoon ground turmeric
1 teaspoon ground red chilli
1–2 teaspoons salt, to taste

## Method

Wash the crab claws thoroughly, using a small brush to get into the tight nooks and remove any dirt. Set them aside to drain.

For the vaghaar, heat the olive oil in a large saucepan over medium heat. Add the cinnamon stick and cloves and fry, giving the pan a swirl now and then, for 1–2 minutes, until their aromas are released. As soon as you start to smell the spices the vaghaar is ready – you don't want to burn the spices.

Add the curry leaves and half the ginger. Once the ginger starts to sizzle, stir in the onion, reduce the heat to low and cover with a lid. Simmer for 8–10 minutes, until the onion has softened and browned. Add the tomato, garlic, chilli, remaining ginger and the spice blend and stir thoroughly. Cover again and simmer, stirring occasionally, for 10–12 minutes.

Meanwhile, crack the crab claws slightly by applying some pressure with your hand or a hard, flat object. Make sure you don't break them – you just want them to be easier to crack and eat once they are cooked.

Crack one of the crab claws open and pick out the crabmeat. Add the crabmeat to the curry sauce, along with the tomato paste. This will add flavour and thicken up the sauce. Cover again and simmer for 5 minutes more, or until the tomato has softened.

Stir in 120–150 ml (4–5 fl oz) of water, add the crab claws, cover and cook for 10–12 minutes.

Remove the cloves and cinnamon stick. Stir in the garam masala and remove the pan from the heat. Squeeze the lemon half over the curry, add the coriander and stir to combine.

Serve with lemon wedges, and naan and/or steamed basmati rice.

# Breads

*Rotli & Naan*

As children, me and my sister would call rotlis 'bhabis', something we later realised was only said in our family. For some reason, you needed to be a certain age to start using the word 'rotli'. On the days we ate Gujarati food it was guaranteed that Mum would make us a little 'sugar bhabi' as a pre-dinner snack – crispier than usual, smothered in butter with a sprinkle of sugar. One of those super simple but unforgettable childhood treats.

Having rotli with a curry is more common than having rice for us, and we always eat with our hands. It might be a slightly foreign concept for some, but don't be afraid to get stuck in there and get your hands a little messy. You can use the bread like a spoon to scoop up the curry!

200ml

# Everyday Rotli

Serves 4 *(Makes 12–15)*

Rotli, or chapati, is a classic staple in West Indian cuisine and my go-to accompaniment for every curry. My mum has this recipe down to a tee and can whip up a batch in under 15 minutes (a record I'm yet to beat). My Maa's speciality is vaghaar nu rotli – if there's any leftover, slightly stale rotli, she shreds it and fries it in a vaghaar until crispy, then serves it with yoghurt. It's a seriously delicious snack.

## Ingredients

375 g (13 oz) atta (whole-wheat) flour,
plus 3 tablespoons, plus extra for dusting

2 tablespoons olive oil, plus 1 teaspoon extra

260 ml (9 fl oz) boiling water, plus extra if needed

butter or ghee, to serve (optional)

## Method

Use a spoon to combine the flour and 2 tablespoons of oil in a large mixing bowl.

Make a well in the flour and add half of the boiling water, then stir to combine. Slowly add the remaining water, stirring until a soft, but not sticky, dough forms. It shouldn't be too dry, so add more boiling water if needed.

Turn the dough out onto your work surface and knead for 5–6 minutes, until it's soft and no longer sticky. Drizzle the 1 teaspoon of oil on the dough and spread it over to cover the surface. You do not need to let the dough rest. Next, divide the dough equally into 12–15 balls.

Add 3 tablespoons of flour to a small bowl. Flatten each ball between your hands to form a small disc, then dip both sides of each disc into the flour.

Lightly dust your work surface, then use a rolling pin to apply a light-medium pressure and roll each disc into a 18 cm (7 in) circle. Try to keep the rotli as round as possible by rolling from different angles and rotating in-between.

Heat a shallow 25 cm (10 in) non-stick frying pan over medium-high heat.

Cook each rotli for 1 minute on each side until it picks up specks of colour. You can use a wooden chapati press or paper towel to apply pressure around the edge of the rotli while turning it to create an air bubble.

Once cooked, stack the rotli in a container with a lid to keep them warm. You can smother the rotli in butter or ghee, if you like, before stacking.

Serve hot with any curry in this book.

# Poori

(Fried Bread)

Serves 4–6 *(Makes 18–20)*

This type of bread isn't for everyday meals and is definitely on the indulgent side, but it's a well-deserved fried treat every now and then. It's about half the size of your classic rotli and is often served at Gujarati weddings. If you love a mix of sweet and savoury, I'd highly recommend dipping the poori into Creamy Doodhpak, Nutty Shrikhand or a tin of store-bought mango raas.

## Ingredients

250 g (9 oz) atta (whole-wheat) flour, plus extra for dusting

1 tablespoon olive oil

80–100 ml (2½–3½ fl oz) boiling water, plus extra if needed

sunflower or vegetable oil, for frying

Batata nu Shaak (page 144) or Creamy Doodhpak (page 248), to serve

## Method

Use a spoon to combine the flour and olive oil in a large mixing bowl.

Make a well in the flour and add the boiling water. Stir until a tough, thick dough forms. It shouldn't be too dry, so add more boiling water if needed.

Turn the dough out onto your work surface and knead for 5–6 minutes, or until firm. You do not need to let the dough rest. Next, divide the dough equally into 18–20 balls.

Flatten each ball between your hands to form a small disc.

Lightly dust your work surface, then use a rolling pin to apply a light–medium pressure and roll each disc into an 8–10 cm (3¼–4 in) circle. Try to keep the poori as round as possible by rolling from different angles and rotating in between.

Heat 5 cm (2 in) of sunflower oil in a large, deep saucepan over medium–high heat. To check the oil is hot enough, drop a little poori dough into the oil – if it sizzles and browns quickly it's hot enough.

Carefully lower two or three pooris into the pan using tongs (how many you can fit in the pan will depend on the size of your pan). Fry the pooris for 1–2 minutes on each side, until golden brown. While the pooris are cooking, prepare a plate lined with paper towel to absorb any excess oil. Remove each cooked poori with tongs and transfer it to the paper towel. Continue until all the pooris are cooked.

Serve with batata nu shaak to accompany dinner or with doodhpak for a sweet treat.

# Yoghurt Naan Bread

Serves 4–6 *(Makes 8–10)*

Naan has always been the ultimate treat bread, usually saved for a weekend curry or a dinner party. It's my favourite bread to indulge in, especially when slathered in butter, and I can't deny it soaks up curry sauce better than rotli. I often buy store-bought naan, but this is a simple, easy way to get your naan fix without needing a tandoor.

## Ingredients

570 g (1 lb 4 oz) self-raising flour, plus extra for dusting

180–200 g (6½–7 oz) Greek or coconut-based yoghurt (see Note)

1½ teaspoons salt

1 tablespoon nigella seeds

1 tablespoon olive oil

roughly chopped coriander (cilantro) leaves and stems, to serve

**Garlic Butter**

3–4 garlic cloves, minced

2–3 coriander (cilantro) sprigs, leaves and stems finely chopped

20 g (¾ oz) room-temperature salted butter or vegan butter

## Method

Combine the flour, yoghurt, salt and nigella seeds in a large mixing bowl to create a rough dough, then stir in the olive oil.

Turn the dough out onto a lightly floured work surface and knead for 5 minutes, or until smooth and elastic. If the dough is too sticky you may need to add more flour. Add more yoghurt if it is too dry.

Divide the dough equally into eight to ten pieces. Lightly dust your work surface with more flour, then roll each piece into an 18–20 cm (7–8 in) oval using a diagonal rolling motion.

For the garlic butter, use a fork to combine the garlic, coriander and butter in a small bowl. (You may need to soften the butter slightly in the microwave.) Set aside.

Heat a non-stick frying pan over medium–high heat.

Dry-fry the dough for roughly 1–2 minutes on each side, until it begins to puff up and the underside browns in places. You can use a wooden chapati press or paper towel to apply pressure around the edge of the naan while turning it to create an air bubble. Continue until all the naan are cooked.

Spread the garlic butter on the naan while they are hot and scatter the coriander on top.

Serve hot with your favourite curry.

**Note**

If using a coconut-based yoghurt, the naans won't puff up when cooking, but they still work and taste just as delicious!

## Yoghurt Naan Bread

Easy to make.
Bowl of self-raising flour,
equal quantity of yoghurt (or try with alternative),
pinch of salt.
x

*Mum*

Just mix everything together,
you'll know how much water to add.
It's like a pancake consistency.

*Mum*

# Poora

(Gluten-free Pancake)

Serves 4 *(Makes 8–10)*

Poora is a great gluten-free alternative made with rice flour, which is packed with protein and fibre. Unlike rotli, this bread starts as a liquid batter rather than a dough – a bit like a pancake. In the Lad household, we usually pair poora with *Dada's Lamb Curry*; the soft texture complements the tender, spicy meat and soaks up the rich curry sauce beautifully.

## Ingredients

250 g (9 oz) rice flour
1 tablespoon gram (besan) flour
2 green chillies, finely chopped
2–3 cm (¾–1¼ in) piece of ginger, grated
½ teaspoon ground turmeric
1 teaspoon salt, to taste
1 egg
sunflower or vegetable oil, for brushing
Dada's Lamb Curry (page 170), to serve

## Method

Whisk the rice flour, gram flour, chilli, ginger, turmeric, salt and egg together in a large mixing bowl. Slowly pour in 400–420 ml (13½–14 fl oz) of water, whisking continuously, until you have a smooth, thin batter.

Heat a shallow 25 cm (10 in) non-stick frying pan over medium heat and brush a thin layer of oil on the surface.

Carefully ladle 60–80 ml (¼–⅓ cup) of batter into the hot pan. Immediately, gently swirl the pan until the batter covers the surface of the whole pan in a thin layer. Cover with a lid and cook for 1–2 minutes. Remove the cover, cook for 2 minutes more, until the pancake is lightly coloured, then flip the poora and cook for 4–5 minutes on the other side without the lid. Continue until all the poora are cooked, making sure to re-brush the pan with oil in between cooking each poora.

Serve with Dada's lamb curry.

# Rice

*Bhat*

Historically, the climate in Gujarat meant the conditions were much more suited to growing wheat than rice. Rotli has long been the main staple to accompany a curry there, and that aspect of the cuisine lives on in Leicester, as we don't often eat rice plated up alongside curries. Instead, rice is a secondary part of the meal – after we've had our rotlis – and it's usually served with any leftover curry sauce poured over it.

I really appreciate the simple pleasure of rice, and often mixing in just a spoonful of butter is all you need. Sometimes less is more. These are a selection of (primarily) simple, delicious rice dishes. The vegetarian and meat biryanis are the only main dishes, and are therefore a bit more of an undertaking, but they're totally worth your time!

# Vaghaar Rice

Serves 4

This is a simple way to spruce up your rice and add a subtle flavour that complements rather than overpowers any curry. You can add in peas to bulk out the rice, add more texture if you like and, if you're feeling indulgent, stir in a spoonful of butter when serving. My mum would always change the way she made rice, rotating between plain rice, vaghaar rice and vegetable rice.

## Ingredients

180 g (6½ oz) basmati rice
1 teaspoon salt
1 white onion, thinly sliced
15 g (½ oz) salted butter or vegan butter
2–3 garlic cloves, minced
1 cm (½ in) piece of ginger, grated
1 green chilli, finely chopped, to taste
100 g (⅔ cup) frozen peas (optional)

**Vaghaar**

1 tablespoon olive oil
1 teaspoon black mustard seeds
1½ teaspoons cumin seeds

**Spice Blend**

½ teaspoon ground turmeric
½ teaspoon ground red chilli
1–2 teaspoons salt, to taste

## Method

Thoroughly wash the rice to remove the starch. Add the uncooked rice to a saucepan, cover it with cold water and use your hands to mix the rice for 20–30 seconds. Drain the cold water and repeat five or six times, until the water starts to run clear.

Next, soak the rice in cold water for 10–15 minutes. Drain, return the rice to the pan and add enough water so that it sits 1–1.5 cm (½ in) above the rice. Add the salt and bring the rice to the boil over medium heat. Once boiling, reduce the heat to low, cover and simmer for 8–10 minutes, until all the water has been absorbed and the rice is cooked.

Meanwhile, for the vaghaar, heat the olive oil in a large saucepan over medium heat. Add the mustard seeds and cumin seeds and fry, giving the pan a swirl now and then, for 1–2 minutes, until the mustard seeds start to pop and sizzle.

Stir in the onion and butter. Once the butter has melted, reduce the heat to low and simmer for 8–10 minutes, until the onion has softened. Stir in the garlic, ginger, chilli and spice blend. Add the peas now too, if using. Cook for 2–3 minutes.

Add the rice and stir to combine, then remove from the heat.

Serve hot as an accompaniment to your favourite saucy curry.

## Quick Veg Rice

Vaghaar oil (mustard seeds and cumin),
fry onions,
add salt,
chilli,
turmeric,
dhana jeera.
Add a little butter …
frozen or fresh veg.
Cook with rice,
add water and cook for 5–10 minutes.
May need to add water.

*Mum*

# Quick Veg Rice

Serves 4

This is a quick weekday alternative to a traditional vegetable biryani – not quite as rich in flavour, but it does the trick. You can use whatever vegetables you have to hand, and it's a great way to use up what's in your fridge and reduce food waste. For ease, I usually use frozen mixed vegetables, which are still packed with plenty of nutrients.

## Ingredients

180 g (6½ oz) basmati rice
1 white onion, thinly sliced
2–3 garlic cloves, minced
1 cm (½ in) piece of ginger, grated
1 green chilli, finely chopped
100 g (3½ oz) mixed frozen vegetables
15 g (½ oz) salted butter or vegan butter

**Vaghaar**
2 tablespoons olive oil
1 teaspoon black mustard seeds
1 teaspoon cumin seeds

**Spice Blend**
1 teaspoon ground coriander
1 teaspoon ground cumin
½ teaspoon ground turmeric
½ teaspoon ground red chilli
1–2 teaspoons salt, to taste

## Method

Thoroughly wash the rice to remove the starch. Add the uncooked rice to a saucepan, cover it with cold water and use your hands to mix the rice for 20–30 seconds. Drain the cold water and repeat five or six times, until the water starts to run clear. Next, soak the rice in cold water for 10–15 minutes.

For the vaghaar, heat the olive oil in a large saucepan over medium heat. Add the mustard seeds and cumin seeds and fry, giving the pan a swirl now and then, for 1–2 minutes, until the mustard seeds start to pop and sizzle.

Stir in the onion, reduce the heat to low and cover with a lid. Simmer for 8–10 minutes, until the onion has softened and browned.

Drain the rice, then stir it into the onion along with the garlic, ginger, chilli, frozen vegetables, spice blend and butter. Cook for 2–3 minutes.

Next, add enough boiling water so that it sits 2 cm (¾ in) above the rice. Cover again and simmer for 10–12 minutes, until the rice is cooked and the water has evaporated. Add more water if needed.

Serve hot as an accompaniment to your favourite saucy curry.

# Kichri

(Rice & Lentils)

Serves 4–6

Each Gujarati cook has their own way of making kichri. Some like it mushy, others add more spices, but my mum makes it very simple, which makes it the perfect remedy for when you're feeling unwell and you need something subtle. It's a comforting rice dish that is soft, mild in flavour and easy to eat. I would pair kichri with a generous ladle of *Kadhi*, a spicy yoghurt gravy.

## Ingredients

120 g (4½ oz) basmati rice
65 g (2¼ oz) mung daal or toor daal
½ teaspoon ground turmeric
1–2 teaspoons salt, to taste
15 g (½ oz) ghee or vegan butter
Kadhi (page 239), to serve

## Method

Thoroughly wash the rice to remove the starch. Add the uncooked rice to a saucepan, cover with cold water and use your hands to mix the rice for 20–30 seconds. Drain the cold water and repeat five or six times, until the water starts to run clear. Next, add the mung daal or toor daal to the rice in the pan and add enough cold water so that it sits 1–1.5 cm (½ in) above the lentils and rice. Soak the rice and lentils for at least 30 minutes.

After soaking, drain the water from the saucepan and add enough boiling water so that it sits 3 cm (1¼ in) above the rice and lentils. Stir in the turmeric and salt.

Bring to the boil over medium heat and cook for 10–12 minutes, until the lentils are cooked. Drain three-quarters of the water out of the pan – leaving just a thin layer at the bottom of the pan. Cover the pan with a lid, reduce the heat to low and simmer for 8–10 minutes more, until the rice is cooked and the water has evaporated.

Stir in the ghee, then serve hot with plenty of kadhi.

# Veg Biryani

Serves 6–8

Here is another gem from Rash Foi, my aunt on my dad's side. Being one of the few vegetarians in the family, she's our go-to for more extravagant vegetarian food. Biryani is a rare dish where rice becomes the main event: no curry required. Feel free to mix in your favourite veggies, and don't skip the potatoes – the double carb is what makes it!

## Ingredients

300 g (1½ cups) basmati rice

1 cinnamon stick

3 whole cloves

2 teaspoons cumin seeds

5–6 cardamom pods

1–2 teaspoons salt, to taste

2–3 small all-purpose potatoes, peeled and cut into 5 mm–1 cm (¼–½ in) thick slices

1 small cauliflower, florets cut off and halved

30 g (2 oz) salted butter, ghee or vegan butter

2 tablespoons olive oil, plus ½ teaspoon extra

1 large white onion, thinly sliced

6 garlic cloves, minced

3–4 cm (1¼–1½ in) piece of ginger, grated

3–4 green chillies, finely chopped, to taste

120 g (4½ oz) frozen peas

120 g (4½ oz) green beans, trimmed and cut into thirds

2 carrots, diced

90 g (⅓ cup) Greek or coconut-based yoghurt

juice of 2 limes

10–15 g (¼–½ oz) coriander (cilantro), leaves and stems roughly chopped

4–5 eggs, hard-boiled and cut into 5 mm thick (¼ in) slices

roasted cashews, whole or crushed, to serve

handful of sultanas (golden raisins), to serve (optional)

**Spice Blend**

1 heaped teaspoon ground coriander

1 heaped teaspoon ground cumin

1 teaspoon ground turmeric

2 teaspoons ground red chilli

1–2 teaspoons salt, to taste

## Method

Thoroughly wash the rice to remove the starch. Add the uncooked rice to a saucepan, cover it in cold water and use yours hands to mix the rice for 20–30 seconds. Drain the cold water and repeat five or six times, until the water starts to run clear. Next, add the cinnamon stick, cloves, cumin seeds, cardamom pods and salt to the pan with enough cold water so that it sits 1–1.5 cm (½ in) above thee. Set aside for 25–30 minutes to soak.

Meanwhile, bring a large saucepan of water to the boil with a sprinkle of salt. Once boiling, add the potato and cauliflower to the pan and boil for 6–8 minutes, until parboiled. Drain and set aside to cool.

After soaking, bring the rice to the boil over high heat in the same water it has been soaking in. Once boiling, reduce the heat to low, cover and simmer for 8 minutes, until all the water has been absorbed and the rice is cooked. Stir in the butter and set aside.

Heat the 2 tablespoons of olive oil in a large saucepan over medium heat. Fry three-quarters of the onion with the garlic, ginger and chilli. Reduce the heat to low and add the parboiled potato and cauliflower, along with the peas, beans, carrot and spice blend, stirring until the vegetables are coated in the spices. Cover and simmer for 6–8 minutes, until the peas have defrosted and the green beans are starting to soften (I like the green beans and carrot to still have some crunch).

Remove from the heat and stir in the yoghurt, lime juice and coriander.

Transfer the mixture to a bowl, leaving a layer of sauce at the bottom of the pan – you will use this pan to assemble the biryani. Set the bowl aside.

Remove the cinnamon stick, cloves and cardamom pods from the rice.

Start to layer the biryani components like a lasagne. Add a layer of rice to the sauce in the pan, then add a layer of the yoghurt mixture, followed by slices of egg. Repeat this layering and finish with a final, thin layer of rice.

Heat the ½ teaspoon of olive oil in a small saucepan over high heat, then fry the remaining quarter of onion for around 5 minutes, until crispy. Sprinkle the crispy onion on top of the rice, along with the cashews and sultanas, if using.

For the best results, leave the biryani to set for a few hours to allow the rice to absorb the flavours. Reheat thoroughly before serving.

**Note**

For the curry, you can use your favourite vegetables or whatever you have to hand.

A lot of faff,
but it's delicious.
Enjoy.
xx

*Rash Foi*

# Sunday Lamb Biryani

Serves 6–8

My mum's lamb biryani is always in high demand – calling it a favourite is an understatement. It's not very traditional, but she has always paired it with a squirt of tomato ketchup on her plate – don't judge until you've tried it! Over the years, the Lad family has developed a unique Christmas tradition: after the classic British roast, we round off the day with biryani – a nice example of cultures colliding.

## Ingredients

900 g (2 lb) lamb leg or shoulder, bone-in (see Notes)

1–2 bay leaves

1 white onion, diced

1½ tomatoes, roughly chopped

½ aubergine (eggplant), roughly chopped

6 garlic cloves, minced

2–3 cm (¾–1¼ in) piece of ginger, grated

1½ green chillies, finely chopped

1 tablespoon tomato paste (concentrated puree)

½ teaspoon garam masala

10–15 g (¼–½ oz) coriander (cilantro), leaves and stems finely chopped, plus extra, to serve

300 g (1½ cups) basmati rice

1 teaspoon ground turmeric

4–5 eggs, boiled and cut into 5 mm (¼ in) thick slices

90 g (⅓ cup) Greek or coconut-based yoghurt

lemon wedges, to serve

**Vaghaar**

2 tablespoons olive oil, plus 2 tablespoons extra

3–4 whole cloves, plus 2–3 extra

½ cinnamon stick, plus 2 extra sticks

2 whole star anise

**Spice Blend**

1 heaped teaspoon ground coriander

1 heaped teaspoon ground cumin

1 teaspoon ground turmeric

½ teaspoon ground red chilli

1–2 teaspoons salt, to taste

**Notes**

You can ask your butcher to prepare the lamb for you.

Want to swap lamb for chicken? Just follow the steps in *Heart-Warming Chicken Curry* (page 166).

If you like, you can add a layer of boiled potato slices to the biryani. Peel and boil 2–3 small sliced potatoes and layer them on top of every layer of egg when building the biryani.

## Method

Cut the lamb into small pieces with the bone in and trim the fat off. Wash the lamb and pat it dry with paper towel.

For the vaghaar, heat 2 tablespoons of the olive oil in a large saucepan over medium heat. Add the 3–4 cloves, ½ cinnamon stick and the star anise and fry, giving the pan a swirl now and then, for 2 minutes, or until their aromas are released. As soon as you start to smell the spices the vaghaar is ready – you don't want to burn the spices.

Stir in the bay leaves and onion, reduce the heat to medium–low and cover with a lid. Simmer for 10 minutes, or until the onion has softened and browned.

Blitz the tomatoes and aubergine together in a food processor to form a puree.

Stir the puree into the pan, along with the garlic, ginger, chilli and spice blend and cover again. Simmer for 8 minutes, stirring occasionally, then stir in the tomato paste. Continue to simmer for 8 minutes more with the lid on, stirring occasionally.

Add the lamb, cover and reduce the heat to low. Cook for 45–60 minutes, until the lamb is tender. If the lamb is starting to stick to the pan, add a little water – however, you want the lamb to absorb the curry sauce and be fairly dry. Stir in the garam masala and remove from the heat. Remove the cloves, cinnamon stick and star anise.

Add the coriander and stir to combine. Set aside.

While the lamb is cooking, prepare the rice.

Thoroughly wash the rice to remove the starch. Add the uncooked rice to a saucepan, cover it with cold water and use your hands to mix the rice for 20–30 seconds. Drain the cold water and repeat five or six times, until the water starts to run clear. Add enough cold water to the pan so that it sits 1–1.5 cm (½ in) above the rice. Set aside for 25–30 minutes.

For the next vaghaar, heat the remaining 2 tablespoons of olive oil in a large saucepan over medium heat. Add 2–3 cloves and 2 cinnamon sticks and fry, giving the pan a swirl now and then, for 1–2 minutes, or until their aromas are released.

Drain the rice and add it into the vaghaar, along with the turmeric, and stir continuously for 2–3 minutes, until the rice starts to stick to the pan.

Add enough boiling water to the saucepan so that it sits 2 cm (¾ in) above the rice. Cover and cook for 8–10 minutes, until all the water has been absorbed and the rice is cooked. Check halfway through and add more water if needed. Remove the cloves and cinnamon sticks from the rice.

Transfer the lamb curry to a bowl, leaving a layer of curry sauce at the bottom of the pan – you will use this pan to assemble the biryani.

Using the same saucepan the curry was cooked in, start to layer the biryani components like a lasagne. Starting with a layer of rice, add a layer of curry, then slices of egg and a drizzle of yoghurt. Repeat this layering and finish with a final, thin layer of rice and scatter with finely chopped coriander.

For the best results, leave the biryani to set for a few hours to allow the rice to absorb the flavours of the curry. Reheat thoroughly before serving with lemon wedges.

# Condiments & Sauces

*Chutney & Achai*

Condiments are never really the main focus of a spread. Still, they're a simple addition that can bring a whole new dimension to a dish. At home, we generally use a mixture of homemade and store-bought condiments, thanks to their wide availability in Leicester's many South Asian shops. My parents always have a jar of store-bought pickled aubergine (eggplant) and lime in the fridge, and microwaved papad (poppadum) are on the table for almost every weekday dinner – a healthier and quicker alternative to frying.

I'd recommend yoghurt-based condiments, such as raita or coconut chutney, for spicy dishes. Mint yoghurt pairs perfectly with meat dishes, especially lamb. Tomato chutney and green chutney make great dipping sauces for starters and snacks, especially those that are fried. And if you're ever short on options, a simple squeeze of lemon almost always enhances a dish.

Homemade condiments tend to be reserved for special occasions, but all the recipes in this chapter are uncomplicated and can be whipped up with little to no fuss.

# Cooling Raita

Serves 4–6

This refreshing and light condiment is the go-to if any starter or main is a little (or much) too spicy. With very little prep time, this raita is an easy shortcut to balancing any Indian meal and sprucing up your dinner table.

## Ingredients

½ teaspoon black mustard seeds
½ long cucumber, grated
350 g (12½ oz) plain or coconut-based yoghurt
½ carrot, grated
½ teaspoon ground cumin
¼ teaspoon garam masala
¼ teaspoon salt
handful of mint leaves, finely chopped
sprinkle of pomegranate seeds (optional)

## Method

Using a mortar and pestle, crush the black mustard seeds to form a fine powder and set aside.

Squeeze all the excess water from the grated cucumber using a paper towel or a thin tea towel.

Combine the yoghurt with the black mustard seed powder, grated cucumber and all the remaining ingredients in a mixing bowl and stir thoroughly.

Store in an airtight container in the fridge for up to 2 days.

# Mint Yoghurt

Serves 4–6

I think mint yoghurt is the ultimate Indian condiment. It's fresh, vibrant and a guaranteed crowd-pleaser. This bright-green dipping sauce brings a burst of colour and flavour to any dinner table. It pairs beautifully with lamb dishes such as *Motiyas* (page 115), *Tray-Baked Lamb Chops* (page 114) and *Keema Pita Breads* (page 111). I think it also tastefully complements almost anything from *Kobi na Motiya* (page 88) to *Spicy Lemon Salmon* (page 179).

## Ingredients

30 g (1 oz) mint leaves (see Note)
20 g (¾ oz) coriander (cilantro) leaves
300 g (10½ oz) Greek or coconut-based yoghurt
½ red onion, finely diced
1 teaspoon ground cumin
¼ teaspoon ground red chilli
½ teaspoon salt

## Method

Blitz the mint and coriander leaves in a food processor with 1–2 tablespoons of water until it forms a fine paste.

Combine the pureed herbs and all the remaining ingredients in a mixing bowl and stir thoroughly.

Store in an airtight container in the fridge for up to 5 days.

**Note**

You can use 1 tablespoon of store-bought mint sauce instead of the mint leaves.

LOADS of coriander and cumin,
pinch of salt.

*Anju Masi*

# Tomato Chutney

Serves 4–6

This chutney tastes best when made with pre-ripe, slightly sour tomatoes and my mum's go-to secret ingredient: a good squeeze of Heinz tomato ketchup. I sometimes add a little raw garlic, but be careful not to overdo it, as it can overpower the flavour. This tangy chutney is an essential whenever I'm making fried treats such as *Mixed Veg Bhajis* (page 78), *Samosas* (pages 94–99) or *Baked Chicken Spring Rolls* (page 102).

## Ingredients

1 tomato, roughly chopped

½ green bell pepper (capsicum), roughly chopped

½ red bell pepper, roughly chopped

1 tablespoon tomato ketchup

10–15 g (¼–½ oz) coriander (cilantro) leaves

1 red chilli, chopped, to taste

1 garlic clove, roughly chopped (optional)

1 teaspoon ground cumin

½ teaspoon salt, to taste

## Method

Blitz all the ingredients in a food processor until you have a puree.

Serve in a small bowl as a dipping sauce. It's best served with fried foods.

Store in an airtight container in the fridge for up to 5 days.

# Fresh Green Chutney

Serves 4–6

This one is for the coriander fans. Most of the recipes in this book are garnished with the peppery herb, but this liquid form is perfect for those who can't get enough. It's less of a dipping sauce and more of a drizzle. I love pouring it over *Baked Handvo* (page 72) or *Fluffy Dhokla* (page 76).

## Ingredients

50 g (1¾ oz) coriander (cilantro) leaves
25 g (1 oz) mint leaves
2 garlic cloves, chopped
1–2 cm (½–¾ in) piece of ginger, chopped
2 green chillies, finely chopped, to taste
juice of ½ lemon
50–80 ml (1¾–2½ fl oz) cold water
1 teaspoon ground cumin
½ teaspoon salt

## Method

Blitz the coriander leaves, mint leaves, garlic, ginger, chilli, lemon juice and 50 ml (1¾ fl oz) of the cold water in a food processor until you have a smooth consistency – add the remaining water if needed.

Stir in the cumin and salt.

Store in an airtight container in the fridge for up to 5 days.

# Coconut Chutney

Serves 4–6

Coconut has to be one of my favourite fruits. It's extremely versatile and is an essential ingredient in many dairy alternatives. Fresh, soft coconut flesh isn't always easy to find, so don't worry if you don't have it to hand; desiccated coconut combined with coconut-based yoghurt is just as tasty. This chutney is often served alongside *Fresh Green Chutney* (page 234) and also pairs perfectly with *Baked Handvo* (page 72) or *Fluffy Dhokla* (page 76).

## Ingredients

300 g (10½ oz) coconut-based yoghurt or plain yoghurt

50 g (1¾ oz) fresh coconut flesh or desiccated coconut

10–15 g (¼–½ oz) coriander (cilantro) leaves

juice of ¼ lemon, to serve

## Method

Blitz the yoghurt, coconut and coriander in a food processor until smooth and creamy.

Serve in a small bowl with a squeeze of lemon.

Store in an airtight container in the fridge for up to 5 days.

# Pickled Onions

Serves 4

Red onions are naturally sweet, which makes them perfect for eating raw. These tangy onions pair perfectly with *Heart-Warming Chicken Curry* (page 166) or *Dada's Lamb Curry* (page 170), adding a crunch and a little extra zing to each mouthful. I like to let them marinate in the balsamic vinegar and lemon juice so that they soften slightly and the flavours deepen.

## Ingredients

1 red onion, thinly sliced
¼ teaspoon salt
½ teaspoon ground black pepper
¼ teaspoon sugar
1 tablespoon balsamic vinegar
juice of ½ lemon

## Method

Combine all the ingredients in a bowl, stirring well, then cover and set aside to allow the onion to marinate at room temperature for at least 30 minutes.

Store in an airtight container in the fridge for up to 2 weeks.

# Sweet & Tangy Apple Chutney

Serves 6–8

This is my maa's favourite chutney – she loves picking at it straight from the jar during lunch or dinner. It's another sweet-and-sour combination, where the sweetness of the apple and the punch of spice pair beautifully with vegetarian curries.

## Ingredients

1 red apple, finely diced with the peel on

juice of ½ lemon

**Vaghaar**

1 tablespoon vegetable oil

½ teaspoon black mustard seeds

¼ teaspoon fenugreek seeds

**Spice Blend**

½ teaspoon ground coriander

½ teaspoon paprika

½ teaspoon ground black pepper

½ teaspoon ground red chilli

½ teaspoon salt, to taste

## Method

Place the diced apple in a sealable jar.

For the vaghaar, heat the vegetable oil in a small saucepan over medium heat. Add the mustard seeds and fenugreek seeds and fry, giving the pan a swirl now and then, for 1–2 minutes, until the mustard seeds start to pop and sizzle and the fenugreek starts to brown. Remove from the heat.

Pour the hot vaghaar over the diced apple, along with the spice blend and lemon juice and give it a quick stir.

Allow the chutney to cool for at least 2 hours – letting the apple soak up the vaghaar and lemon juice – before sealing and placing it in the fridge.

Store in the fridge for up to 10 days.

# Kadhi

(Yoghurt Gravy)

Serves 4

This spicy yoghurt gravy is the perfect quick midweek fix, adding a little zing to *Kichri* or steamed basmati rice. Kadhi is yoghurt-based, so it complements almost any curry – don't worry about mixing flavours on your plate.

## Ingredients

60 g (¼ cup) plain or coconut-based yoghurt

1 teaspoon gram (besan) flour

2 garlic cloves, minced

1 cm (½ in) piece of ginger, grated

1 green chilli, finely chopped

150 ml (5 fl oz) cold water

coriander (cilantro), leaves and stems roughly chopped, to serve

steamed basmati rice or Kichri (page 214), to serve

**Vaghaar**

1 teaspoon cumin seeds

1 tablespoon ghee or vegan ghee

5–6 curry leaves

**Spice Blend**

½ teaspoon ground coriander

½ teaspoon ground cumin

½ teaspoon ground turmeric

1–2 teaspoons salt, to taste

## Method

Whisk the yoghurt, flour, garlic, ginger, chilli, spice blend and cold water together in a bowl until you get a soupy consistency.

For the vaghaar, heat the cumin seeds in a saucepan over medium heat and dry-fry for 1–2 minutes, until they are browned and fragrant. Add the ghee and curry leaves and cook for 4–5 minutes, until the ghee has melted.

Reduce the heat to medium–low and stir in the yoghurt mixture. Continue to stir for 5 minutes, or until the yoghurt is heated through. Remove the pan from the heat and add the coriander. Serve hot with kichri or steamed rice.

You can store leftovers in an airtight container in the fridge for up to 5 days.

# Maa's Daal

(Sweet-and-sour Gravy)

Serves 4–6

This is my grandma's speciality and a beloved staple from my dad's childhood. My mum has spent years trying to recreate it, but somehow it never tastes quite the same. We always keep a tub of Maa's daal tucked away in the freezer for emergencies. Surprisingly, the secret is a generous squeeze of tomato ketchup and plenty of sugar to strike that perfect sweet-and-sour balance.

## Ingredients

100 g (3½ oz) toor daal

boiling water

1 tomato, roughly chopped

2–3 cm (¾–1¼ in) piece of ginger, roughly chopped

2½ green chillies, roughly chopped

1 tablespoon goor (jaggery) or brown sugar, to taste

juice of ¼ lemon

1 tablespoon tomato ketchup

steamed basmati rice, to serve

**Vaghaar**

1 tablespoon olive oil

1 teaspoon black mustard seeds

1 teaspoon cumin seeds

½ teaspoon fenugreek seeds

2 dried whole red chillies

5–6 curry leaves

pinch of asafoetida

**Spice Blend**

1 teaspoon ground coriander

1 teaspoon ground cumin

¼ teaspoon ground turmeric

¼ teaspoon ground red chilli

1–2 teaspoons salt, to taste

## Method

Soak the toor daal in a saucepan of cold water for 30–40 minutes.

Drain the water off the toor daal and add enough boiling water so that it sits 2 cm (¾ in) above the toor daal. Bring to the boil over medium heat, then reduce the heat to low, cover and simmer for 35–40 minutes, until the toor daal are very soft and break easily. You want a yellow, watery consistency. Do not drain.

Meanwhile, blitz the tomato, ginger and chilli in a food processor until pureed. Add the puree, along with the spice blend, goor, lemon juice and ketchup, to the toor daal and stir to combine. Bring to the boil again for 2–3 minutes to allow the goor to melt. Remove from the heat and use a hand-held blender to blend until smooth.

For the vaghaar, heat the olive oil in a small saucepan over medium heat. Add the mustard seeds, cumin seeds, fenugreek seeds, dried red chillies, curry leaves and asafoetida. Fry, giving the pan a swirl now and then, for 2 minutes, or until the mustard seeds start to pop and sizzle and the fenugreek starts to brown. Pour the hot vaghaar over the daal and stir to combine.

Serve over rice and eat after your main curry.

# Desserts

## *Mithai*

As kids, Mum made sure we ate healthily, and dinner would always be followed by a variety of chopped fruit (a home comfort I often miss). This was particularly good during mango season in India, when mangoes are imported to the UK and fill up the Indian grocery stores here. Mum and Dad still won't buy them any other time of year.

For that reason, Indian desserts were never a big part of Mum's repertoire. I wanted to include a mango raas recipe in this book – a kind of mango soup sprinkled with cumin – but Mum said, 'no one makes it, it comes out of a tin.' I was a little surprised, but I guess it's unfair to expect her to know how to make everything!

Most Indian desserts contain lots of cardamom, so feel free to adjust the amount to suit your taste. Unfortunately, they also contain copious amounts of ghee, which most of the time can't be substituted for a dairy-free alternative. I associate this chapter with both of my maas (grandmas), as the dishes evoke memories of indulging in sweet treats such as doodhpak (rice pudding) and mithi seviyan (sweet vermicelli noodles) at their houses.

# Creamy Doodhpak (Rice Pudding)

Serves 4–6

Doodhpak, also known as 'kheer' in many Indian cultures, is a creamy sweet treat that is traditionally made for special occasions such as Diwali (the festival of light) and Holi (the festival of colour).

Don't worry if you're dairy-intolerant, it works just as well with oat, almond or coconut milk, and it even cooks in half the time, which is a nice bonus.

## Ingredients

60 g (2 oz) short-grain rice

1 tablespoon canola (rapeseed) or sunflower oil (optional)

1.15 litres (39 fl oz) full-cream (whole) milk or plant-based milk (see Note)

80–100 ml (2½–3½ fl oz) double (heavy) cream or vegan cream (optional)

2 heaped tablespoons white or brown sugar, to taste

10 cardamom pods, crushed to a fine powder using a mortar and pestle

**To Serve**

thinly sliced pistachios

thinly sliced almonds

Poori (page 196)

## Method

Add the uncooked rice to a saucepan and wash it five or six times under cold running water until the water starts to run clear. Drain, return the rice to the pan and add warm water to cover. Soak the rice for 30 minutes.

Drain the water from the saucepan, leaving the rice in the pan, then add enough cold water to just cover the rice. Cook over high heat for 2–3 minutes, then add 1 tablespoon of oil (you don't need to do this if you're using alternative milk, as that already contains oil) to coat the bottom of the saucepan – this will prevent the milk from burning and the rice from sticking to the base of the pan.

Slowly pour the milk into the pan while stirring. Keep stirring until the milk starts to boil, then reduce the heat to low and simmer for 30–40 minutes, stirring continuously, until the milk starts to thicken. The milk will reduce by half and the rice will be more visible in the mixture.

Next, stir in the cream, if using, sugar and cardamom powder. Stir for 2–3 minutes more, until the sugar has dissolved, then remove from the heat.

Serve warm, sprinkled with sliced pistachios and almonds alongside some poori for dipping into the pudding.

**Note**

You can use oat, almond or coconut milk instead of dairy milk; however, the cooking time will be halved. You will only need to stir the milk and rice for around 20 minutes.

# Mithi Seviyan

(Sweet Vermicelli)

Serves 6–8

Sweet noodles may sound unusual, but they really do work. Traditionally made with wheat vermicelli, you can also make them with rice vermicelli for a gluten-free version. I love the sticky texture and simplicity of this dish – best enjoyed with a sprinkle of your favourite nuts and dried fruits for extra crunch and flavour.

## Ingredients

60–70 g (2–2½ oz) vermicelli noodles (rice or wheat)

15–20 g (½–¾ oz) salted butter, ghee or vegan ghee

230 ml (8 fl oz) milk or plant-based milk

230 ml (8 fl oz) boiling water

handful of pistachios, sliced, plus extra to serve

handful of almonds, sliced, plus extra to serve

handful of cashews, sliced, plus extra to serve

180 g (6½ oz) caster (superfine) sugar, to taste

6–8 cardamom pods, crushed to a fine powder using a mortar and pestle

## Method

Break up the vermicelli noodles into smaller strands in a bowl.

Heat the butter in a saucepan over low heat until it melts completely. Add the vermicelli and stir frequently, to prevent it from burning, for 4–5 minutes, or until the vermicelli starts to brown.

Add the milk and boiling water, making sure the vermicelli is covered in the liquid – add more water if needed. Cook for 2–3 minutes, then stir in the sliced nuts.

Cook for 5–6 minutes more, stirring, until the vermicelli starts to soften, then stir in the sugar and cardamom powder. Continue to cook, stirring, for 5 minutes more, until the liquid has reduced and been absorbed by the vermicelli.

Serve warm with extra sliced nuts.

# Nutty Shrikhand

(Dessert Yoghurt)

Serves 4

Shrikhand is often served alongside a main meal, where you can alternate mouthfuls between sweet and savoury. It goes particularly well with hot *Poori*. I love frozen yoghurt, so sometimes I like to pop a small bowl of shrikhand in the freezer for 45–60 minutes to firm it up, giving it that ice cream–like texture. As with most Indian desserts, you can serve it with your favourite nuts, though pistachios are a must!

## Ingredients

2–3 saffron strands

1 tablespoon milk or plant-based milk, warmed

handful of pistachios

handful of almonds

350 g (12½ oz) Greek or coconut-based yoghurt

3 tablespoons sugar, to taste

3–4 cardamom pods, crushed to a fine powder using a mortar and pestle

Poori (page 196), to serve (optional)

## Method

Combine the saffron and warm milk in a bowl and set aside.

Blitz the nuts in a food processer briefly to form a rough nut mix – don't process them too much.

Whisk the yoghurt and sugar together in a mixing bowl until you get a smooth, creamy consistency. Add the saffron-soaked milk and cardamom powder and whisk again.

Cover the bowl and refrigerate for at least 30 minutes.

Serve, sprinkled with the pistachios and almonds, alongside some hot poori, if you like.

**Note**

The shrikhand will keep in the fridge for up to 3 days.

# Seero

(Creamy Semolina)

Serves 6–8

Seero, a dessert traditionally prepared for religious celebrations, is known for its soft texture and melt-in-the-mouth sweetness. It's often given out at the mandir (Hindu temple) as prasad, a devotional food offering made to the Gods and later shared among devotees. I learnt this recipe from Anju Masi (my mum's sister), and her golden rule is simple: never stop stirring.

## Ingredients

500 ml (2 cups) milk

200 g (7 oz) ghee

200 g (7 oz) coarse semolina

80–100 g (2¾–3½ oz) sugar, to taste

10 cardamom pods, crushed to a fine powder using a mortar and pestle

thinly sliced almonds, to serve

green raisins, to serve

## Method

Add the milk to a saucepan and place it on the stovetop. Don't turn on the heat yet.

Heat the ghee in a separate saucepan over low heat until it melts completely. Add the semolina and keep stirring for 8 minutes. Keep stirring the semolina while you turn the heat on low for the milk to slowly heat up. After 5 minutes, whisk the sugar into the milk until it dissolves. Keep the milk on a very low heat until you need it. Keep stirring the semolina for 2–5 minutes more, or until it starts to lighten in colour and the ghee floats on top of the mixture – this means it's time to add the milk.

Slowly pour the milk into the semolina while continuing to stir. If the mixture starts to bubble, take the pan off the heat for a few seconds. Keep stirring for 3–4 minutes, until you have a soft, sticky texture that holds its form when moulded. Remove from the heat and stir in the cardamom powder.

Serve the seero hot with a sprinkle of almonds and raisins.

**Note**

You can serve seero with your favourite nuts – pistachios, cashews and walnuts are all delicious with this creamy semolina.

# Sweet & Crispy Malpua

(Gujarati Pancakes)

Serves 4–6 *(Makes 18–20)*

This recipe brings back fond memories of my late maa. It was one of her favourite sweet treats, and it never feels quite the same eating this dish without her. Malpua are crispier and chewier than Western-style pancakes, and served without toppings. They are often made on religious days in Gujarati households and are best enjoyed with a glass of cold milk.

## Ingredients

200 g (7 oz) goor (jaggery) or brown sugar (see Note)

4–5 cardamom pods

6–8 whole cloves

2 teaspoons fennel seeds

240 g (8½ oz) atta (whole-wheat) flour

2–3 tablespoons ghee or vegan ghee

sunflower or vegetable oil, for frying

**To Serve**

vanilla ice cream

white poppy seeds (khus khus; available from Indian grocery stores)

chopped pistachios

## Method

Soak the goor in 400 ml (13½ fl oz) of lukewarm water in a mixing bowl for 5 minutes.

Use your hands to break the goor up in the water until it completely dissolves – you now have sugar syrup. Do not use boiling water or heat the goor over a flame or in a microwave.

Using a mortar and pestle, crush the cardamom pods and cloves into a fine powder.

Combine the powdered spices, fennel seeds and flour in a large mixing bowl. Slowly pour the goor syrup into the bowl while whisking until you have a medium-consistency batter. It shouldn't be too runny or too thick – add more water if needed.

Cover and set the batter aside to ferment for 4–6 hours at room temperature. After resting, if the batter is too thick, add a little more water.

When you are ready to make the malpua, heat the ghee and 2–3 cm (¾–1¼ in) of oil in a deep frying pan over high heat. To check the oil is hot enough, drop a little batter into the oil – if it sizzles and browns quickly it's hot enough.

Carefully ladle 2–3 tablespoons of batter into the pan and use the back of a spoon to quickly spread it out to form an 8–10 cm (3¼–4 in) pancake. The thinner the batter, the easier it will spread in the oil. Fry the malpua for 2–3 minutes on each side, until it darkens in colour and crisps up. While the malpua is cooking, prepare a plate lined with paper towel to absorb any excess oil. Remove the cooked malpua with tongs and transfer it to the paper towel. Continue until all the malpuas are cooked.

Serve the malpuas hot with vanilla ice cream, topped with white poppy seeds and pistachios.

**Note**

If using brown sugar, you need to make a sugar syrup. Whisk together the sugar and 400 ml (13½ fl oz) of water in a saucepan over medium heat until it comes to boiling point. Reduce the heat to low and simmer, stirring continuously, for 1–2 minutes, until the sugar is completely dissolved.

# Gajar na Halwa (Sweet Carrot Pudding)

Serves 6–8

My all-time favourite Indian dessert – and the one I miss most since becoming dairy intolerant. It was taught to me by my family friend Rachna Kaki, who never turns up to a get-together without a dessert in hand. Slowly cooking the carrots in sweet milk completely transforms their flavour and texture, turning them rich, sticky and perfectly sweet. Serve it warm with a scoop of vanilla ice cream. Simply irresistible!

## Ingredients

300 g (10½ oz) large carrots

3 tablespoons ghee, plus extra for spreading

285 ml (9½ fl oz) milk or plant-based milk

145 g (⅔ cup) caster (superfine) sugar, to taste

100 g (1 cup) milk powder

3–4 cardamom pods, crushed to a fine powder using a mortar and pestle

pinch of freshly grated nutmeg

handful of pistachios, thinly sliced

handful of almonds, thinly sliced

handful of cashews, thinly sliced

vanilla ice cream, to serve

## Method

Grate the long side of the carrots, discarding the tough middle part.

Heat 2 tablespoons of the ghee in a large saucepan over low heat until melted. (It's important to keep the pan on low heat throughout this recipe to prevent burning the ghee.) Add the grated carrot and continue stirring for 8–10 minutes, until the carrot starts to soften.

Next, add the milk and continue to stir for 12–15 minutes, until the liquid has been absorbed and the carrot has lightened in colour.

Stir in the sugar, then gradually add the milk powder while continuing to stir. Keep stirring for 3–4 minutes more, until the consistency thickens. Add the remaining 1 tablespoon of ghee and stir for another 3–4 minutes, until the ghee has melted. Remove from the heat.

Spread a layer of ghee onto the bottom of a shallow serving dish. Transfer the hot carrot mixture into the dish, then sprinkle the cardamom powder, nutmeg and nuts on top.

Serve warm with vanilla ice cream.

# Nankhatai

(Cardamom Cookies)

Serves 10–12 *(Makes 18–20)*

No surprise here, it's another Gujarati dessert flavoured with cardamom! If you're not a fan, don't worry, these cookies are just as delicious without the spice. This recipe was taught to me by my Moti Kaki (aunt on my dad's side). The cookies are traditionally bite-sized, though I sometimes like to make them larger. Their melt-in-your-mouth, crumbly texture is to die for, especially with a hot cup of *Morning Masala Chai* (page 49).

## Ingredients

110 g (4 oz) ghee or vegan ghee, plus extra if needed

100 g (3½ oz) icing (confectioners') sugar

3–4 cardamom pods, crushed to a fine powder using a mortar and pestle

½ teaspoon natural vanilla extract

½ teaspoon natural almond extract

110 g (¾ cup) plain (all-purpose) flour

40 g (1½ oz) gram (besan) flour

40 g (1½ oz) coarse semolina

2 tablespoons crushed pistachios

## Method

Preheat the oven to 180°C (350°F) and line a baking tray with baking paper.

Beat the ghee and icing sugar together in a large mixing bowl until fluffy and light.

Add the cardamom powder, vanilla extract and almond extract to the bowl and stir to combine.

Sift the plain flour, gram flour and semolina into the bowl, then stir it through with a spoon to create a stiff dough. You may need to add more ghee to ensure the ingredients combine.

Roll 18–20 small round balls and place them on the baking tray.

Use the bottom of a glass to flatten the balls slightly, then use a knife to mark a light cross on top of each cookie. Next, sprinkle the crushed pistachios over each cookie and gently press the nuts into the dough.

Bake for 10–12 minutes, until light golden brown. Set aside to cool.

The cookies will keep stored in an airtight container for up to 2 weeks.

## Thank You

This project has been six years (on and off) in the making and I couldn't have done it without my amazing mum (of course). Firstly, I want to say a huge thank you to her, not only for providing the recipes, but for being a constant support, cooking countless dishes multiple times and patiently enduring my nagging for precise measurements and instructions. And to my dad, Ram, the primary taste-tester, who was always full of ideas, would happily run around Leicester to find me last-minute ingredients and is the co-photographer behind many images. I'll let you both cook in peace now!

A special thank you to my partner, Leo, who shared and understood my vision and story from the beginning and beautifully put my thoughts into written words. Your continuing patience, support and feedback (on every meal, photograph and design) has been invaluable and I couldn't have done this without you.

Thank you to the talented women in my wider family who shared and taught me a few recipes that Mum and I knew you were better at. A huge thank you to my family, friends and colleagues who have been cheerleaders along the way and took the time to test out the recipes. I am forever grateful.

Finally, to my grandparents – who bravely journeyed overseas many years ago, leaving behind family, memories and home, but carrying with them an imprint of every delicious recipe. I hope I've made you proud!

Maa (Paliben) Cooking on Holiday
Portugal, 1990s

Dada (Nanubhai), Me & Maa (Paliben)
Checketts Close Kitchen, Leicester

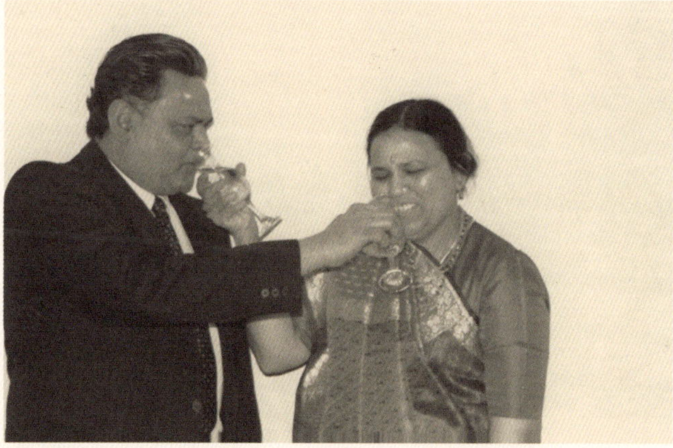

Dada (Ranchhodbhai) & Maa (Manjulaben)
25th Wedding Anniversary, 1990s

Me & Mum (Mina)
Shanklin Avenue Kitchen, Leicester

# Index

## S



## T



## V



## Y

Smith
Street
Books

Published in 2026 by Smith Street Books
Naarm (Melbourne) | Australia
smithstreetbooks.com

Distributed outside of ANZ, North & Latin America by
Thames & Hudson Ltd., 6–24 Britannia Street, London, WC1X 9JD
thamesandhudson.com

EU Authorised Representative: Interart S.A.R.L.
19 rue Charles Auray, 93500 Pantin, Paris, France
productsafety@thameshudson.co.uk; www.interart.fr

ISBN: 978-1-9235-0337-3



Smith Street Books respectfully acknowledges the Wurundjeri People of the Kulin Nation, who are the Traditional Owners of the land on which we work, and we pay our respects to their Elders past and present.



Publisher: Megan Cuthbert
Additional text: Leo Gonzalez
Managing editor: Lucy Heaver
Editor: Martine Lleonart
Design, layout and photography: Alissa Lad
Proofreader: Pamela Dunne
Production manager: Aisling Coughlan

Printed & bound in China by C&C Offset Printing Co., Ltd.

Book 478
10 9 8 7 6 5 4 3 2 1

FSC
www.fsc.org
MIX
Paper | Supporting responsible forestry
FSC® C008047